3

Literacy
Through Texts

PEARSON
Longman

Lorna Hendry • Roger Lane
Lucy Lawrence • Steve Ridgway

Contents

Key:

 pair work activity    group work activity    achievement target

 ICT   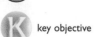 single person activity

R revision objective   K key objective

Further activities and support can be found on the Companion Website at www.longman.co.uk/literacythroughtexts

1 The gothic tradition

Before you read: looking at visual texts

Look at the two photographs. Answer the questions and think about what we mean by the term 'gothic'.

1 a) Describe the building in the first picture. You should refer to its size, shape, colour and the historical period it represents.

   b) What atmosphere is created in this picture?

   c) What features of the visual image create this atmosphere?

2 What events do you think might happen in this building?

3 a) Describe the atmosphere created by this second picture.

   b) What aspects of the picture create this atmosphere?

4 a) What fictional events might take place in a location like this?

5 Consider both pictures.

   a) What do they have in common?

   b) Which genre would you say they belong to?

6 List the possible features of the **genre** that these pictures belong to.

1.1 Dracula: novel and screenplay

Dracula: the novel

This extract is taken from the novel *Dracula* by Bram Stoker written in 1897. Here Dr John Seward, Professor Van Helsing, Quincey Morris and Arthur Holmwood have just entered the tomb of Lucy Westenra, Arthur's fiancée. Lucy has recently died in unusual circumstances. One of the men, Professor Van Helsing, suspects that there is something sinister going on and consequently has called upon Seward, Morris and Holmwood to help him to uncover the truth.

Before you read

This novel is written in a diary form. What other diaries have you read? With a partner, discuss and list the features you might expect to encounter in diary writing.

Dracula: Dr Seward's Diary

'There was a long spell of silence, a big aching void, and then from the Professor a keen 'Ss-s-s!' He pointed; and far down the avenue of yews we saw a white figure advance – a dim white figure, which held something dark at its breast. The figure stopped, and at the moment a ray of moonlight fell between the masses of driving clouds and showed in startling prominence a dark-haired woman, dressed in the cerements of the grave. We could not see the face, for it was bent down over what we saw to be a fair-haired child. There was a pause and a sharp little cry, such as a child gives in sleep, or a dog as it lies before the fire and dreams. We were starting forward, but the Professor's warning hand, seen by us as he stood behind a yew-tree, kept us back; and then as we looked the white figure moved forward again. It was now near enough for us to see clearly, and the moonlight still held. My own heart grew cold as ice, and I could hear the gasp of Arthur as we recognized the features of Lucy Westenra. Lucy Westenra, but yet how changed. The sweetness was turned to adamantine, heartless cruelty, and the purity to voluptuous wantonness. Van Helsing stepped out, and obedient to his gesture, we all advanced too; the four of us ranged in a line before the door of the tomb. Van Helsing raised his lantern and drew the slide; by the concentrated light that fell on Lucy's face we could see that the lips were crimson with fresh blood, and that the stream had trickled over her chin and stained the purity of her lawn death-robe.

We shuddered with horror, I could see by the tremulous light that even Van Helsing's iron nerve had failed. Arthur was next to me, and if I had not seized his arm and held him up, he would have fallen.

When Lucy – I call the thing that was before us Lucy because it bore her shape – saw us she drew back with an angry snarl, such as a cat gives when taken unawares; then her eyes ranged over us. Lucy's eyes in form and colour; but Lucy's eyes unclean and full of hell-fire, instead of the pure, gentle orbs we knew. At that moment the remnant of my love passed into hate and loathing; had she then to be killed, I could have done it with savage delight. As she looked, her eyes blazed with unholy light, and the face became wreathed with a voluptuous smile. Oh, God, how it made me shudder to see it! With a careless motion, she flung to the ground, callous as a devil, the child that up to now she had clutched strenuously to her breast, growling over it as a dog growls over a bone. The child gave a sharp cry, and lay there moaning. There was a cold-bloodedness in the act which wrung a groan from Arthur; when she advanced to him with outstretched arms and a wanton smile, he fell back and hid his face in his hands.

She still advanced, however, and with a languorous[1], voluptuous grace, said:

'Come to me, Arthur. Leave these others and come to me. My arms are hungry for you. Come, and we can rest together. Come, my husband, come!'

There was something diabolically[2] sweet in her tones – something of the tingling of glass when struck – which rang through the brains even of us who heard the words addressed to another. As for Arthur, he seemed under a spell; moving his hands from his face, he opened wide his arms. She was leaping for them, when Van Helsing sprang forward and held between them his little golden crucifix. She recoiled from it, and, with a suddenly distorted face, full of rage, dashed past him as if to enter the tomb.

When within a foot or two of the door, however, she stopped as if arrested by some irresistible force. Then she turned, and her face was shown in the clear burst of moonlight and by the lamp, which had now no quiver from Van Helsing's iron nerves. Never did I see such baffled malice[3] on a face; and never, I trust, shall such ever be seen again by mortal eyes. The beautiful colour became livid, the eyes seemed to throw out sparks of hell-fire, the brows were wrinkled as though the folds of the flesh were the coils of Medusa's snakes, and the lovely, bloodstained mouth grew to an open square, as in the passion masks of the Greeks and Japanese. If ever a face meant death – if looks could kill – I saw it at that moment.

1 Drooping   2 Inhumanely cruel   3 Ill will

And so for full half a minute, which seemed an eternity, she remained between the lifted crucifix and the sacred closing of her means of entry. Van Helsing broke the silence by asking Arthur:

'Answer me, oh my friend! Am I to proceed in my work?'

Arthur threw himself on his knees, and hid his face in his hands, as he answered:

'Do as you will, friend; do as you will. There can be no horror like this ever any more!' and he groaned in spirit. Quincey and I simultaneously moved towards him, and took his arms. We could hear the click of the closing lantern as Van Helsing held it down; coming close to the tomb, he began to remove from the chinks some of the sacred emblems which he had placed there. We all looked on in horrified amazement as we saw, when he stood back, the woman, with a corporeal[1] body as real at the moment as our own, pass in through the interstice where scarce a knife-blade could have gone. We all felt a glad sense of relief when we saw the Professor calmly restoring the strings of putty to the edges of the door.

When this was done, he lifted the child and said:

'Come now, my friends; we can do no more till to-morrow. There is a funeral at noon, so here we shall all come before long after that. The friends of the dead will all be gone by two, and when the sexton lock the gate we shall remain. Then there is more to do; but not like this of to-night. As for this little one, he is not much harm, and by to-morrow night he shall be well. We shall leave him where the police will find him, as on the other night; and then to home.' Coming close to Arthur, he said:

'My friend Arthur, you have had sore trial; but after, when you will look back you will see how it was necessary. You are now in the bitter waters, my child. By this time to-morrow, you will, please God, have passed them, and have drunk of the sweet waters; so do not mourn overmuch. Till then I shall not ask you to forgive me.'

Arthur and Quincey came home with me, and we tried to cheer each other on the way. We had left the child in safety, and were tired; so we all slept with more or less reality of sleep.

Reading for meaning

1 The reader's first impression of Lucy in the distance is one of innocence, symbolised by the description of her as a 'white figure'. How does the author change the reader's idea about Lucy? Use quotations from the text to support your answer.

2 Lucy tries to persuade Arthur to embrace her. How does she do this and why do you think Van Helsing acts as he does to prevent this from happening?

3 Why do you think Van Helsing brought Arthur, Lucy's fiancé, to witness these events? By the end of the extract, what does Arthur realise?

4 The extract is taken from the diary of one of the characters involved in the tale. What is unusual about the narrative style used in this diary entry?

The **narrative** voice is the perspective from which a text is written. There are two main narrative perspectives used, the **first-person narrative**, which uses 'I' and 'me', and the **third-person narrative**, which uses 'he' and 'they'. The effect generated by using these different narrative voices can be quite dramatic.

- What is the narrative voice used in diary writing? Why is this appropriate? What effect is created by using this perspective?

Vocabulary and spelling

1 Find the word 'adamantine' in the text (paragraph 1). In pairs, discuss the meaning of this word. Look at the context of its use and consider its sound. Finally, check the meaning in a dictionary.

2 a) Find modern equivalents for the expression used to describe the clothes that Lucy is wearing, the 'cerements of the grave' (paragraph 1).

b) Compare the nineteenth-century expression with the modern expression and say why the phrase used is more suited to this text.

Homonyms are words which have the same spelling, but different meanings. For example: 'bear' can mean 'a large carnivorous animal' or it can mean 'to carry a load'.

- In pairs, list five other homonyms and give their different meanings.

Homophones are words that have the same sound, but different spelling and meaning. For example: 'there', 'they're', 'their' all sound the same, but have different spellings and meanings.

- Study the following words and give the homophone and meaning for each.

  waist   allowed   peace   through   great   break

Now read on...

29 September, night – A little before twelve o'clock we three – Arthur, Quincey Morris, and myself – called for the Professor. It was odd to notice that by common consent we had all put on black clothes. Of course, Arthur wore black, for he was in deep mourning, but the rest of us wore it by instinct. We got to the churchyard by half-past one, and strolled about, keeping out of official observation, so that when the gravediggers had completed their task, and the sexton, under the belief that everyone had gone, had locked the gate, we had the place all to ourselves. Van Helsing, instead of his little black bag, had with him a long leather one, something like a cricketing bag; it was manifestly of fair weight.

When we were alone and had heard the last of the footsteps die out up the road, we silently, and as if by ordered intention, followed the Professor to the tomb. He unlocked the door, and we entered, closing it behind us. Then he took from his bag the lantern, which he lit, and also two wax candles, which, when lighted, he stuck, by melting their own ends, on other coffins, so that they might give light sufficient to work by. When he again lifted the lid off Lucy's coffin we all looked – Arthur trembling like an aspen – and saw that the body lay there in all its death-beauty. But there was no love in my own heart, nothing but loathing for the foul Thing which had taken Lucy's shape without her soul. I could see even Arthur's face grow hard as he looked. Presently he said to Van Helsing:

'Is this really Lucy's body, or only a demon in her shape?'

'It is her body, and yet not it. But wait a while, and you shall see her as she was, and is.'

She seemed like a nightmare of Lucy as she lay there; the pointed teeth, the bloodstained, voluptuous mouth – which it made one shudder to see – the whole carnal and unspiritual appearance, seeming like a devilish mockery of Lucy's sweet purity. Van Helsing, in his methodical manner, began taking the various contents from his bag and placing them ready for use. First he took out a soldering iron and some plumbing solder, and then a small oil-lamp; which gave out, when lit in a corner of the tomb, gas which burned at fierce heat with a blue flame, then his operating knives, which he placed to hand; and last a round wooden stake, some two and a half or three inches thick and about three feet long. One end of it was hardened by charring in the fire, and sharpened to a fine point. With this stake came a heavy hammer, such as in households is used in the coal-cellar for breaking the lumps. To me, a doctor's preparations for work of any kind are stimulating and bracing, but the effect of these things on both Arthur and Quincey was to cause them a sort of consternation. They both, however, kept their courage and remained silent and quiet.

When all was ready, Van Helsing said:

'Before we do anything, let me tell you this; it is out of the lore and experience of the ancients and of all those who have studied the powers of the Un-Dead. When they become such, there comes with the change the curse of immortality; they cannot die, but must go on age after age adding new victims and multiplying the evils of the world; for all that die from the preying of the Un-Dead become themselves Un-Dead, and prey on their kind. And so the circle goes on ever widening, like as the ripples from a stone thrown in the water. Friend Arthur, if you had met that kiss which you know of before poor Lucy die; or again, last night when you open your arms to her, you would in time, when you had died, have become *nosferatu*, as they call it in Eastern Europe, and would all time make more of those Un-Deads that so have filled us with horror. The career of this so unhappy dear lady is but just begun. Those children whose blood she suck are not as yet so much the worse; but if she live on,

Un-Dead, more and more they lose their blood, and by her power over them they come to her; and so she draw their blood with that so wicked mouth. But if she die in truth, then all cease; the wounds of the throats disappear, and they go back to their plays unknowing ever of what has been. But of the most blessed of all, when this now Un-Dead be made to rest as true dead, then the soul of the poor lady whom we love shall again be free. Instead of working wickedness by night and growing more debased in the assimilation of it by day, she shall take her place with the other Angels. So that, my friend, it will be a blessed hand for her that shall strike the blow that sets her free. To this I am willing; but is there none amongst us who has a better right? Will it be no joy to think of hereafter in the silence of the night when sleep is not: "It was my hand that sent her to the stars; it was the hand of him that loved her best; the hand that of all she would herself have chosen, had it been to her to choose"? Tell me if there be such a one amongst us.'

We all looked at Arthur. He saw, too, what we all did, the infinite kindness which suggested that his should be the hand which would restore Lucy to us as a holy, and not an unholy, memory; he stepped forward and said bravely, though his hand trembled, and his face was as pale as snow:

'My true friend, from the bottom of my broken heart I thank you. Tell me what I am to do, and I shall not falter!' Van Helsing laid a hand on his shoulder, and said:

'Brave lad! A moment's courage, and it is done. This stake must be driven through her. It will be a fearful ordeal – be not deceived in that – but it will be only a short time, and you will then rejoice more than your pain was great; from this grim tomb you will emerge as though you tread on air. But you must not falter when once you have begun. Only think that we, your true friends, are round you, and that we pray for you all the time.'

'Go on,' said Arthur hoarsely. 'Tell me what I am to do.'

'Take this stake in your left hand, ready to place the point over the heart, and the hammer in your right. Then when we begin our prayer for the dead – I shall read him. I have here the book, and the others shall follow – strike in God's name, that so all may be well with the dead that we love, and that the Un-Dead pass away.'

Reading for meaning

1 The three friends respond very differently to the contents of Van Helsing's 'cricketing bag'.

 a) What are the contents of this bag and what is the Professor's attitude as he takes them out of his bag?

 b) How do Seward, Morris and Holmwood respond to what the Professor is doing?

2 Lucy is one of the Un-Dead, a vampire.

 a) What are the characteristics of an Un-Dead?

 b) How did Lucy become one of these creatures?

3 How do you think Lucy will be released, given the collection of instruments which Van Helsing has brought?

Read on ...

Arthur took the stake and the hammer, and when once his mind was set on action his hands never trembled nor even quivered. Van Helsing opened his missal and began to read, and Quincey and I followed as well as we could. Arthur placed the point over the heart, and as I looked I could see its dint in the white flesh. Then he struck with all his might.

The Thing in the coffin writhed; and a hideous, blood-curdling screech came from the opened red lips. The body shook and quivered and twisted in wild contortions; the sharp white teeth champed together till the lips were cut and the mouth was smeared with a crimson foam. But Arthur never faltered. He looked like a figure of Thor as his untrembling arm rose and fell, driving deeper and deeper the mercy-bearing stake, whilst the blood from the pierced heart welled and spurted up around it. His face was set, and high duty seemed to shine through it; the sight of it gave us courage, so that our voices seemed to ring through the little vault.

And then the writhing and quivering of the body became less, and teeth ceased to champ, and the face to quiver. Finally it lay still. The terrible task was over.

The hammer fell from Arthur's hand. He reeled and would have fallen had we not caught him. Great drops of sweat sprang out on his forehead, and his breath came in broken gasps. It had indeed been an awful strain on him; and had he not been forced to his task by more than human considerations he could never have gone through with it. For a few minutes we were so taken up with him that we did not look towards the coffin. When we did, however, a murmur of startled surprise ran from one to the other of us. We gazed so eagerly that Arthur rose, for he had been seated on the ground, and came and looked too; and then a glad, strange light broke over his face and dispelled altogether the gloom of horror that lay upon it.

There in the coffin lay no longer the foul Thing that we had so dreaded and grown to hate that the work of her destruction was yielded as a privilege to the one best entitled to it; but Lucy as we had seen her in her life, with her face of unequalled sweetness and purity. True that there were there, as we had seen them in life, the traces of care and pain and waste; but these were all dear to us, for they marked her truth to what we knew. One and all we felt that the holy calm that lay sunshine over the wasted face and form was only an earthly token and symbol of the calm that was to reign for ever.

Van Helsing came and laid his hand on Arthur's shoulder, and said to him:

'And now Arthur, my friend, dear lad, am I not forgiven?'

The reaction of the terrible strain came as he took the old man's hand in his, and raising it to his lips, pressed it, saying:

'Forgiven! God bless you that you have given my dear one her soul again, and me peace.' He put his hands on the Professor's shoulder, and laying his head on his breast, cried for a while silently, whilst we stood unmoving. When he raised his head Van Helsing said to him:

'And now, my child, you may kiss her. Kiss her dead lips if you will, as she would have you to, if for her to choose. For she is not a grinning devil now – not any more a foul Thing for all eternity. No longer she is the devil's Un-Dead. She is God's true dead, whose soul is with Him!'

Arthur bent and kissed her, and then we sent him and Quincey out of the tomb; the Professor and I sawed the top off the stake, leaving the point of it in the body. Then we cut off the head and filled the mouth with garlic. We soldered up the leaden coffin, screwed on the coffin-lid, and gathering up our belongings, came away. When the Professor locked the door he gave the key to Arthur.

Outside the air was sweet, the sun shone, and the birds sang, and it seemed as if all nature were tuned to a different pitch. There was gladness and mirth and peace everywhere, for we were at rest ourselves on one account, and we were glad, though it was with a tempered joy.

Before we moved away Van Helsing said:

'Now, my friends, one step of our work is done, one the most harrowing to ourselves. But there remains a greater task: to find out the author of all this our sorrow and to stamp him out. I have clues which we can follow; but it is a long task, and a difficult, and there is danger in it, and pain. Shall you not all help me? We have learned to believe, all of us – is it not so? And since so, do we not see our duty? Yes! And do we not promise to go on to the bitter end?'

Each in turn, we took his hand, and the promise was made. Then said the Professor as we moved off:

'Two nights hence you shall meet with me and dine together at seven of the clock with friend John. I shall entreat two others, two that you know not as yet; and I shall be ready to all our work show and our plans unfold. Friend John, you come with me home, for I have much to consult about, and you can help me. To-night I leave for Amsterdam, but shall return to-morrow night. And then begins our great quest. But first I shall have much to say, so that you may know what is to do and to dread. Then our promise shall be made to each other anew; for there is a terrible task before us, and once our feet are on the ploughshare, we must not draw back.'

The **gothic novel** of the late eighteenth century featured accounts of terrifying experiences in ancient castles. These experiences were set in dungeons, secret passageways and graveyards. An innocent heroine inevitably suffered at the hands of an evil villain. The term '**gothic**' developed to represent the mysterious, the fantastic, the supernatural and, particularly, the terrifying.

Reading for meaning

1 Arthur drives the stake through Lucy's heart. Why is it appropriate that he should be the one who performs this deed?

2 Read the first three paragraphs on page 12 again. This description of Arthur driving the stake through his beloved Lucy's heart has a powerful effect on the reader. How would you describe this effect? How does Bram Stoker achieve this effect?

3 What does Arthur's reaction to completing this deed tell you about his character?

4 Read the following section again:

Arthur bent and kissed her, and then we sent him and Quincey out of the tomb; the Professor and I sawed the top off the stake, leaving the point of it in the body. Then we cut off the head and filled the mouth with garlic. We soldered up the leaden coffin, screwed on the coffin-lid, and gathering up our belongings, came away.

  a) Why do you think that the author describes the act of driving the stake through Lucy's heart in such vivid terms and yet, when Van Helsing completes the task, there is no such vivid description?

  b) Compare the descriptions of these two gory acts. What different techniques does the author employ? Use quotation from the text to support your comments.

5 Reread pages 5 and 6 up to the point when Lucy dashes into the tomb. How does the author create and build tension in this scene? *Hint: You should consider setting, actions and vocabulary choice, as well as grammatical techniques and sentence construction.*

6 This chapter looks at the gothic style. Which aspects or features of Bram Stoker's *Dracula* are part of the gothic tradition?

Vocabulary

W 7

> The **connotation** of a word differs from the **denotation** of a word.
> Connotation is the **implied** or suggested meaning of a word. Denotation is
> the **actual** meaning of a word.
> For example: The **denotation** or actual meaning of the word 'green' is the
> colour. The **connotation** of 'green' can be envy, or natural and good.

1 Look through the section you read in question 5 on page 15.
   Comment on the connotation and denotation of the colours used.

2 The author describes Lucy's brows as if they '*were wrinkled as though
   the folds of the flesh were the coils of Medusa's snakes*'. Later on, he
   refers to Arthur as looking '*like a figure of Thor*'. Medusa and Thor are
   both characters from ancient mythology.

   a) Find out as much as you can about both these mythological
      characters.

   b) What is the connotation of the imagery of 'the coils of Medusa's
      snakes' and the 'figure of Thor'?

   c) Write a paragraph in which you compare the use of these images
      as a description for that character.

   d) Using images from your own experience and knowledge, create
      two expressions to describe the characters of Van Helsing and
      Dracula.

Drama

*'Two nights hence you shall meet with me and dine together at seven of
the clock with friend John. I shall entreat two others, two that you
know not as yet; and I shall be ready to all our work show and our
plans unfold.'*

In groups of four or six, improvise the conversation which takes place at
this dinner. In your preparation, you should consider:

* the personality of the character you are playing

* the events which have led up to this dinner

* what the problem is

* what course of action needs to be taken.

Writing to inform, explain and describe

Sn 7

> Good information writing uses a variety of different techniques to entertain and educate its audience. The features typically used in this **genre** of writing are called **stylistic conventions**.
>
> • In pairs, collect five examples of information writing. Discuss and list the main features of this type of writing. You should think about the audience, the layout, the language and style used, the purpose, and the different types of approach used.

A new series of books is going to be published which provides comprehensive information on a variety of different subjects from birds to weaponry. The series is directed at ten to fourteen year-olds and aims to inform through use of both text and image.

One book in this series is to be called 'The Gothic Tradition'.

Your task is to produce two pages for this book on one of the most famous of all gothic villains, the vampire. Using the Bram Stoker extracts, as well as any other relevant information you can find, put together two pages of text and illustrations as a double-page spread.

Some suggestions for the type of information to include are:

- their origins
- how to recognise a vampire
- different types of vampire
- where vampires live
- what their habits are
- how to get rid of them.

For your final piece, you should consider the layout of your pages, the balance between text and image, the use of diagrams and text boxes, the use of font and colour.

Bram Stoker's Dracula: the screenplay

The story of Dracula has been adapted for the cinema screen for almost a hundred years. The following extract comes from the 1992 screenplay, written by James V. Hart, for *Bram Stoker's Dracula*, a film directed by Francis Ford Coppola. The extract is taken from the actual filmscript.

Dracula Screenplay

Bram Stoker's Dracula: J. V. Hart

❧⟡❧

London, September 1897

[London street – night]
Dracula's pixilation POV[1]
Through crowd, building tension, ending in close two shot of Mina and Harker through the hansom window.

DRACULA (OS)[2]
(angry animal whisper)
She belongs to me –

We see Harker turn and react, sensing Dracula's presence.

Harker's POV – Dracula
(Music cue.) Standing full view in the light of the street lamps, looking right at Harker!

Younger than Harker remembers him.

[Hansom window – continuing action]

Harker stands; his legs buckle. Mina catches him, cradling him down. His eyes wild in terror and amazement.

MINA
Jonathan? What is it?

HARKER
It is the man himself! He has grown young!

[Hillingham cemetery – night]

Low-angle tracking shot (maze)[3]
With the feet of men approaching the crypt.
Fog rolls in.

Medium close shot
Lamps flash across the iron gate leading to the family crypt. Holmwood reluctantly unlocks the gate. Van Helsing leads them in.

[Crypt – night]

1 POV	Camera shot taken from a particular point of view	
2 Offscreen (OS)	An event that take place out of view of the camera	
3 Tracking shot	A camera shot that follows the movement of an object or character	

19

High wide angle[1]

The men enter. It is very cold. The coffin sits on a stone altar. Seward and Quincey inspect it with their lamps.

HOLMWOOD

Must we desecrate poor Lucy's grave? She died horribly enough –

Medium close-up Van Helsing

VAN HELSING

If – Miss Lucy is dead – there can be no wrong done to her. But if she is not –

HOLMWOOD

My God, what are you saying – has she been buried alive?

VAN HELSING

All I say is that she is "un-dead".

Two shot[2] Seward and Quincey unscrewing the top of the coffin.

Medium close-up Holmwood
He is an emotional mess.

HOLMWOOD

This is insanity.

Overhead shot

looking down on coffin. Van Helsing prises the lead flange back. As Quincey and Seward remove the lid, the camera pulls slowly back so that when they open it, we see a wide shot of the empty coffin.

Past Van Helsing on Holmwood

HOLMWOOD

Where is she?

He pulls out a pistol, levelling it at Van Helsing.

HOLMWOOD

(screams)

Where is she! What have you done with her?

Over pistol on Van Helsing

VAN HELSING

(calm)

---

1 High wide angle   A camera shot taken from a high level, taking in the whole scene
2 Two shot   A camera shot that contains two people

She lives beyond the grace of God. A wanderer in the outer darkness. She is "Vampyre". "Nosferatu". These creatures do not die like the bee after the first sting – but instead grow strong and become immortal once infected by another "nosferatu".

(pushes pistol aside)

So, my friends, we fight not just one beast – but legions, that go on age after age, feeding on the blood of the living.

Soft feminine singing drifts into the vault. Holmwood recognises the voice. He shrinks back – Van Helsing signals. Seward shuts off the lantern.

Wide shot

The men hide near a side wall.

Men's POV–Lucy

in her bridal gown, descending the stairs.

She holds a young child at her breast, singing a lullaby, swaying –

View on the men

They react. Holmwood openly gasps.

Back to men's POV of Lucy

We pan her to the coffin. Van Helsing steps out flanked by the others, and calls to her.

Medium shot[1] of Lucy

She turns, and we see her feeding on the child, her lips and gown fresh with a tiny stream of blood. She sees the men, drops the child carelessly, and steps back.

View on men

Their horrified reaction

Medium shot child

on the ground. It moans, crying. Seward enters the frame, picks it up – checking its condition.

Two shot – Holmwood and Quincey

Holmwood buckles. Quincey is horrified and aroused at the same time but ready with his rifle –

Tracking with Lucy

She transforms to the beautiful, virginal Lucy. She approaches Holmwood with a voluptuous grace.

---

1 Medium shot   A camera shot that includes head and upper body

LUCY

**Come to me, Arthur. Leave these others and come to me. My arms
are hungry for you. Come, and we can rest together. Come, my
husband, come –**

Back to Holmwood
approaching her in a trance; we track in front of him a little as he opens his
arms –

HOLMWOOD
Lucy –

Van Helsing jumps between them, raising his crucifix –

Medium close Lucy
(Stoker: "She recoiled from it. Her face was shown in the clear burst of
moonlight and by the lamp. ...If ever a face meant death – if looks could kill
– we saw it at that moment.")

We track with Van Helsing, forcing Lucy back.

Reading for meaning

1 At the beginning of this extract, the script suggests that it is 'building
   tension'. How is tension created in this opening shot of the scene?

2 What do you notice about the amount of dialogue used in this section
   of the script? Is this balance of dialogue to direction what you
   expected? Explain your response.

3 When a character does speak in this extract, the dialogue is often
   accompanied by a voice direction which indicates the manner in which
   the words should be said.

   Consider why the scriptwriter does not include direction on every
   occasion.

4 Again within the dialogue, the scriptwriter uses dashes on a number of
   occasions. For what purpose are these punctuation marks used? Look
   at the end of the extract.

5 Music is used in the opening moments of this scene, but the script does
   not identify what type of music. What music would you use and why?

Close up	A camera shot that contains the whole head only
Long shot	A camera shot taking in the whole scene from a distance
Low angle shot	A camera shot taken from low level, looking up
Mise en scène	The visual elements of the scene. For example: coffin, stone altar
Panning shot	A camera shot that sweeps in an arc from one side to the other
Snap focus	A sudden sharp focus on something

Film language

R 7

1 In what ways would you say that this filmscript differs from:

a) a playscript

b) a piece of prose, for example novel or short story?

2 Take a section of the filmscript and make a thorough analysis of the language used, its meaning and effect on the audience. You should refer to the camera work, mise en scène, lighting, sound, and dialogue where relevant. What direction would you add which has not already been included?

Writing to imagine, explore and entertain

The scene in the filmscript leads into the one in which Arthur Holmwood drives a stake through Lucy's heart as she lies in her coffin. Read the corresponding section of the novel again, starting 'Arthur took the stake …' on page 12.

In the same groups you used for question 2 in *Film language*, script the film version of this incident. You should use the same stylistic conventions which you studied when looking at the novel.

1.2   Love and gothic

In this short story by Charles Baudelaire, the author uses the fact that different people respond to the same scene in different ways to describe how love turns to hate.

The Eyes of the Poor

Ah! You want to know why I hate you today. It will undoubtedly be harder for you to understand than for me to explain: for you must be the finest example one could find of female impenetrability.

We had passed a long day together which had seemed short to me. We had promised each other that we would share all our thoughts, and that from now on our two souls would be as one: – not a very original dream, after all, even though it is dreamed by all men and achieved by none.

In the evening you were rather tired, and wanted to sit down in a new café on the corner of a new boulevard still covered with debris, which was already displaying its uncompleted splendour. The café was sparkling. The very gas shone with the eagerness of a newcomer, lighting up with all its strength the walls that blinded us with their whiteness, the dazzling surface of the mirrors, the gold on the mouldings and the cornices[1], the pages with their chubby cheeks dragged along by dogs on a lead, the ladies smiling at a falcon perched on their fist, the nymphs and the goddesses carrying fruits, pâté and game on their heads, the Hebes and the Ganymedes with arms stretched out offering little jars of sweetmeats or an obelisk of multicoloured ices – the whole history, the whole mythology, in the service of gluttony[2].

Right in front of us, on the roadway, stood a worthy man of forty-odd with a grizzled beard: he looked tired, and held a little boy with one hand, while on the other arm he carried a tiny creature too weak to walk. He was their nursemaid, bringing the children out to take the evening air. They were all in rags. The three faces were strikingly earnest, and the six eyes stared at the new café with the same wonder, but subtly differentiated by age.

1 A decorative plaster moulding around a ceiling
2 Eating more than you need

24

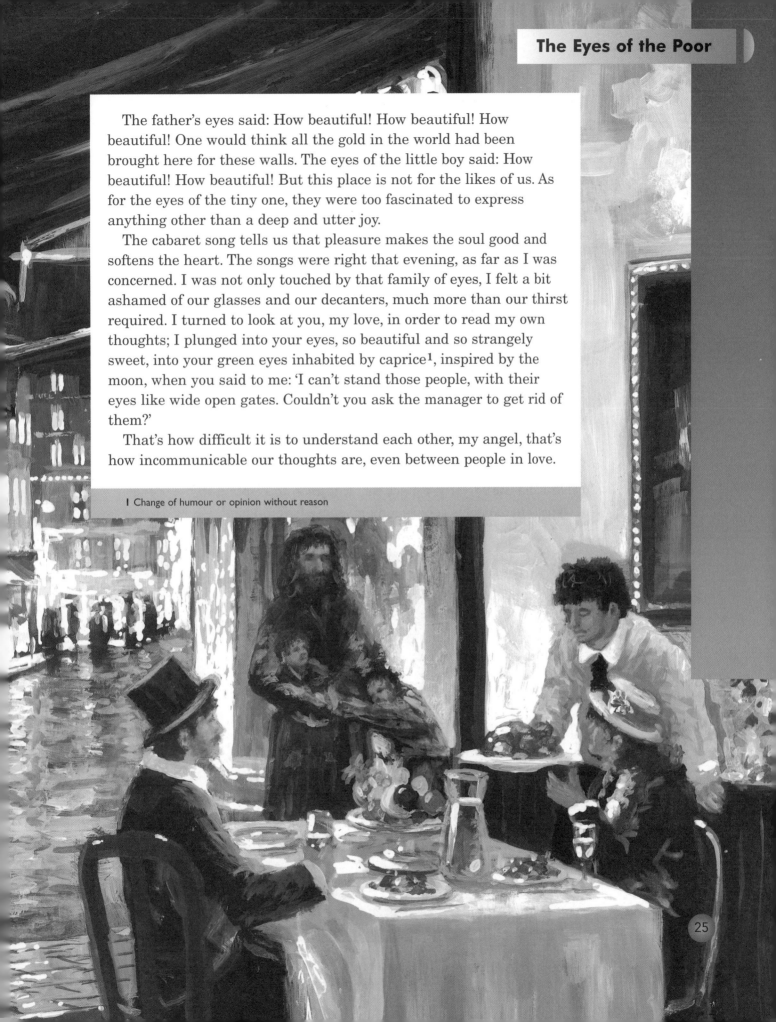

The father's eyes said: How beautiful! How beautiful! How beautiful! One would think all the gold in the world had been brought here for these walls. The eyes of the little boy said: How beautiful! How beautiful! But this place is not for the likes of us. As for the eyes of the tiny one, they were too fascinated to express anything other than a deep and utter joy.

The cabaret song tells us that pleasure makes the soul good and softens the heart. The songs were right that evening, as far as I was concerned. I was not only touched by that family of eyes, I felt a bit ashamed of our glasses and our decanters, much more than our thirst required. I turned to look at you, my love, in order to read my own thoughts; I plunged into your eyes, so beautiful and so strangely sweet, into your green eyes inhabited by caprice[1], inspired by the moon, when you said to me: 'I can't stand those people, with their eyes like wide open gates. Couldn't you ask the manager to get rid of them?'

That's how difficult it is to understand each other, my angel, that's how incommunicable our thoughts are, even between people in love.

1 Change of humour or opinion without reason

Reading for meaning

1 a) When do you think this story was written?

   b) Where does the incident take place?

   c) Why do you think this?

2 a) Who is the narrator talking to?

   b) What do we learn about both characters? What is their relationship?

3 In what terms does the narrator describe the new café? You should use quotations from the text to support your answer.

4 When the family group is mentioned, the father is described as 'worthy'. Consider what else is said about the family, and decide what you think Baudelaire means by this expression.

5 Compare the narrator's response to the new café and the response of the family to the new café. Why do you think there is a difference in attitude?

6 How did the narrator expect his companion to respond to the scene? What effect did his companion's response have on him?

How Beautiful You Are

In this poem, Robert Smith (right) takes the situation described in the Baudelaire short story and adapts it for his own use in a song. Smith wrote this poem for The Cure in 1992.

Research

1 'How Beautiful You Are' and 'Subway Song' are songs written by Robert Smith for a band called The Cure. Using the Internet, find out as much as you can about the band's style and the type of music they played.

2 In what ways do you think this band was influenced by the gothic tradition?

Robert Smith

Before you read: looking at visual texts

Working in groups, study the two photographs carefully. These individuals belong to the gothic sub-culture.

1 What do you notice about the 'look' these individuals are trying to achieve? How do they achieve this 'look'? You should comment on the clothing, the hair, the body art and anything else you consider relevant.

2 Discuss your expectations of and response to these individuals.

3 Why do you think that they adopted the 'tag' gothic? In what ways do they fit in with the gothic tradition?

How Beautiful You Are

You want to know why I hate you?
Well I'll try and explain …
You remember that day in Paris
When we wandered through the rain
And promised to each other
That we'd always think the same
And dreamed that dream
To be two souls as one
And stopped just as the sun set
And waited for the night
Outside a glittering building
Of glittering glass and burning light …
And in the road before us
Stood a weary greyish man
Who held a child upon his back
A small boy by the hand
The three of them were dressed in rags
And thinner than the air
And all six eyes stared fixedly on you
The father's eyes said 'Beautiful!
How beautiful you are!'
The boy's eyes said
'How beautiful!

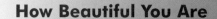

She shimmers like a star!'
The child's eyes uttered nothing
But a mute and utter joy
And filled my heart with shame for us
At the way we are
I turned to look at you
To read my thoughts upon your face
And gazed so deep into your eyes
So beautiful and strange
Until you spoke
And showed me understanding is a dream
'I hate these people staring
Make them go away from me!'
The father's eyes said 'Beautiful!
How beautiful you are!'
The boy's eyes said
'How beautiful! She glitters like a star!'
The child's eyes uttered joy
And stilled my heart with sadness
For the way we are
And this is why I hate you
And how I understand
That no-one ever knows or loves another
Or loves another

Robert Smith

R 7

Reading for meaning

1 Robert Smith has adapted Baudelaire's story into song lyrics. In order to make the poem effective, what changes has he made to:

- story
- setting
- form
- meaning?

2 Rather than the richness and plenty of the food and wine, what does this author choose to focus on in his poem? Why do you think he does this?

3 In both texts each author encourages the reader to respond to the characters differently. Looking at both texts:

a) how do we respond to the narrator's companion

b) how do both authors manage to create this response?

4 Approximately one hundred years separate the two versions of this story. Why do you think Robert Smith chose this particular story to adapt into song lyrics?

5 This was written as a media text, a song. What impact has this had upon the content and style of the text?

Wr 3

Sn 9

Writing to analyse, review and comment

Write a formal essay in which you compare Baudelaire's short story and Smith's song, looking at the content, language and style. Which of these pieces is more effective? Explain your reasons for saying so. You should use standard English and spend 35 minutes on this.

Wr 5

Writing to imagine, explore and entertain

Baudelaire and Smith have both written the story in the first-person narrative, as if they were addressing another person, talking about the events which happened when they were together.

Using the same narrative technique, rewrite the story from the point of view of the narrator's companion. Describe the experience from her point of view, explaining how she felt and why she reacted in the way she did.

1.3 Subterranean gothic

Subway Song

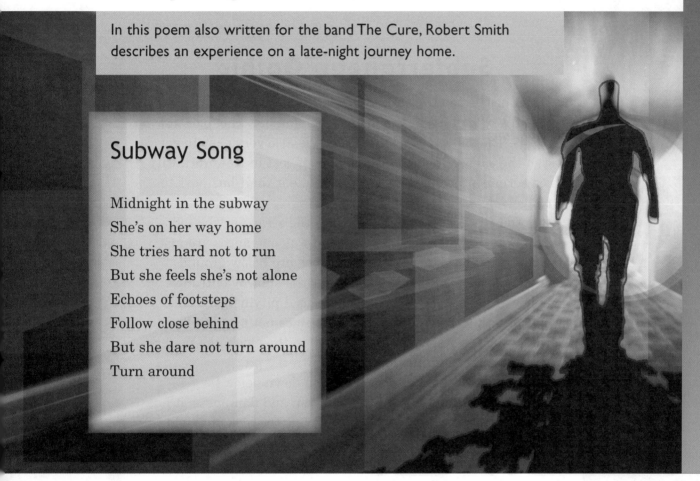

In this poem also written for the band The Cure, Robert Smith describes an experience on a late-night journey home.

Subway Song

Midnight in the subway
She's on her way home
She tries hard not to run
But she feels she's not alone
Echoes of footsteps
Follow close behind
But she dare not turn around
Turn around

Reading for meaning

1 What emotions is the woman in the song experiencing as she makes her way home? Give evidence from the text.

2 What mood does the author create? How does he do this?

3 What effect does the repetition of the words 'turn around' have on the reader?

4 What, if any, of the features of this song could you say are of the gothic tradition?

Some writing is factual but begins to take on a surreal air when the author colours his prose by taking stylistic elements from the gothic tradition.

In this extract by Paul Theroux, he travels on the New York subway … 'a serious matter – the rackety train, the silent passengers, the occasional scream.'

Subterranean Gothic

When people say the subway frightens them, they are not being silly or irrational. It is no good saying how cheap or how fast it is. The subway is frightening. It is also very easy to get lost in the subway, and the person who is lost in New York City has a serious problem. New Yorkers make it their business to avoid getting lost.

It is the stranger who gets lost. It is the stranger who follows people hurrying into the stair-well; subway entrances are just dark holes in the sidewalk – the stations are below ground. There is nearly always a bus stop near the subway entrance. People waiting at a bus stop have a special pitying gaze for people entering the subway. It is sometimes not pity, but fear, bewilderment, curiosity, or fatalism; often they look like miners' wives watching their menfolk going down the pit.

The stranger's sense of disorientation down below is immediate. The station is all tile and iron and dampness; it has bars and turnstiles and steel grates. It has the look of an old prison or a monkey cage.

Buying a token, the stranger may ask directions, but the token booth – reinforced, burglar-proof, bulletproof – renders the reply incoherent. And subway directions are a special language: 'A train … Downtown … Express to the Shuttle … Change at Ninety-sixth for the two … Uptown … The Lex … CC … LL ... The Local …'

Most New Yorkers refer to the subway by the now-obsolete forms **'IND', 'IRT', 'BMT'**. No one intentionally tries to confuse the stranger; it is just that, where the subway is concerned, precise directions are very hard to convey.

Verbal directions are incomprehensible, written ones are defaced. The signboards and subway maps are indiscernible beneath layers of graffiti… .

Graffiti is destructive; it is anti-art; it is an act of violence, and it can be deeply menacing. It has displaced the subway signs and maps, blacked-out the windows of the trains and obliterated the instructions. *In case of emergency* – is cross-hatched with a felt-tip. *These seats are for the elderly and disabled* – a yard-long signature obscures it. *The subway tracks are very dangerous; if the train should stop, do not* – the rest is black and unreadable. The stranger cannot rely on printed instructions or warnings, and there are few cars out of the six thousand on the system in which the maps have not been torn out. Assuming the stranger has boarded the train, he or she can feel only panic when, searching for a clue to his route, he sees in the map-frame the message, **Guzmán**[1] – *Ladrón, Maricón y Asesino.*

Panic: and so he gets off the train, and then his troubles really begin.

He may be in the South Bronx or the upper reaches of Broadway on the Number 1 line, or on any one of a dozen lines that traverse Brooklyn. He gets off the train, which is covered in graffiti, and steps on to a station platform which is covered in graffiti. It is possible (this is true of many stations) that none of the signs will be legible. Not only will the stranger not know where he is, but the stairways will be splotched and stinking – no *Uptown*, no *Downtown*, no *Exit*. It is also possible that not a single soul will be around, and the most dangerous stations – ask any police officer – are the emptiest. …

This is the story that most people tell of subways fear. In every detail it is like a nightmare, complete with rats and mice and a tunnel and a low ceiling. It is manifest suffocation, straight out of Poe[2]. Those who tell this story seldom have a crime to report. They have experienced fear. It is completely understandable – what is worse than being trapped underground? – but it has been a private horror. In most cases, the person will have come to no harm. He will, however, remember his fear on that empty station for the rest of his life.

1 Abimael Guzmán, leader of the Peruvian terrorist group Shining Path
2 Edgar Allan Poe (1809–49) was one of America's greatest writers, especially famous for his tales of terror.

Reading for meaning

1 Paul Theroux describes the subway as something 'straight out of Poe'.

a) In what ways is the subway frightening?

b) What expressions create that sense of fear?

c) How is this similar to the writing of Bram Stoker?

2 What does Paul Theroux consider to be the most frightening aspect of subway travel in New York? Explain your reasons for choosing this aspect and support your comments with reference to text.

3 What is unusual about the fear experienced by the subway traveller?

4 a) What narrative style is being used in this piece of writing?

b) What is the effect of using this approach?

5 Some of the graffiti is written in Spanish.

a) What does this tell us?

b) What do the words mean?

c) What effect do these words have on the traveller?

Now read on ...

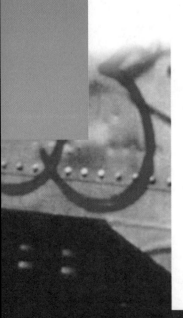

When New Yorkers recount an experience like this they are invariably speaking of something that happened on another line, not their usual route. Their own line is fairly safe, they'll say; it's cleaner than the others; it's got a little charm, it's kind of dependable; they've been taking it for years. Your line has crazy people on it, but my line has 'characters'. This sense of loyalty to a regularly used line is the most remarkable thing about the subway passenger in New York. It is, in fact, a jungle attitude.

In any jungle, the pathway is a priority. People move around New York in various ways, but the complexities of the subway have allowed the New Yorker to think of his own route as something personal, even original. No one uses maps on the subway – you seldom see any.

Reading for meaning

1 In the extract on page 34 Paul Theroux refers to the subway as a jungle. In what ways is this an appropriate comparison to make? How does the author follow this image through?

2 What is unusual about the narrative technique used by Theroux in these two paragraphs?

Now read on ...

Most subway passengers were shown how to ride it by parents or friends. Then habit turns it into instinct, just like a trot down a jungle path. The passenger knows where he is going because he never diverges from his usual route. But that is also why, unless you are getting off at precisely his stop, he cannot tell you how to get where you're going.

In general, people have a sense of pride in their personal route; they may be superstitious about it and even a bit secretive. Vaguely fearful of other routes, they may fantasise about them – these 'dangerous' lines that run through unknown districts. This provokes them to assign a specific character to the other lines. The IRT is the oldest line; for some people it is dependable, with patches of elegance (those beaver mosaics at Astor Place), and for others it is dangerous and dirty. One person praises the IND, another person damns it. 'I've got a soft spot for the BMT,' a woman told me, but found it hard to explain why. 'Take the A train,' I was told. 'That's the best one, like the song.' But some of the worst stations are on the (very long) A line. The CC, 8th Avenue local, was described to me as 'scuzz' – disreputable – but this train, running from Bedford Park Boulevard, the Bronx, via Manhattan and Brooklyn, to Rockaway Park, Queens, covers a distance of some thirty-two miles. The fact is that for some of these miles it is pleasant and for others it is not. There is part of one line that is indisputably bad; that is the stretch of the 2 line (IRT) from Nostrand to New Lots Avenue. It is dangerous and ugly and when you get to New Lots Avenue you cannot imagine why you went. The police call this line 'The Beast'.

But people in the know – the police, the Transit Authority, the people who travel throughout the system – say that one line is pretty much like another.

No line is entirely good or bad, crime-ridden or crime-free. The trains carry crime with them, picking it up in one area and bringing it to another. They pass through a district and take on the characteristics of that place. The South Bronx is regarded as a high-risk area, but seven lines pass through it, taking vandals and thieves all over the system. There is a species of vandalism that was once peculiar to the South Bronx: boys would swing on the stanchions – those chrome poles in the centre of the car – and, raising themselves sideways until they were parallel with the floor, they would kick hard against a window and break it. Now this South Bronx window-breaking technique operates throughout the system. This business about one line being dependable and another being charming and a third being dangerous is just jungle talk.

The most-mugged man in New York must be the white-haired creaky-looking fellow in Bedford–Stuyvesant who has had as many as thirty mugging attempts made on him in a single year. And he still rides the subway trains. He's not as crazy as he looks: he's a cop in the Transit Police, a plain-clothes man who works with the Mobile Task Force in the district designated 'Brooklyn North'. This man is frequently a decoy. In the weeks before Christmas he rode the J and the GG and the 2 lines looking like a pathetic senior citizen, with two gaily-wrapped parcels in his shopping bag. He was repeatedly ambushed by unsuspecting muggers, and then he pulled out his badge and handcuffs and arrested his attackers.

Muggers are not always compliant. Then the Transit Police Officer unholsters his pistol, but not before jamming a coloured headband over his head to alert any nearby uniformed officer. Before the advent of headbands many plain-clothes men were shot by their colleagues in uniform.

'And then we rush in,' says Sergeant Donnery of the Mobile Task Force. 'Ninety per cent of the guys out there can kick my ass, one on one. You've got to come on yelling and screaming. "You so-and-so! You so-and-so! I'm going to kill you!" Unless the suspect is deranged and has a knife or something. In that case you might have to talk quietly. But if the guy's tough and you go in meek you get sized up very fast.'

The Transit Police has three thousand officers and thirteen dogs. It is one of the biggest police forces in the United States and is altogether independent from the New York City Police, though the pay and training are exactly the same. It is so independent the men cannot speak to each other on their radios, which many Transit Police find inconvenient when chasing a suspect up the subway stairs into the street.

What about the dogs? 'Dogs command respect,' I was told at Transit Police Headquarters. 'Think of them as a tool, like a gun or a nightstick. At the moment it's just a test programme for high-crime stations, late-night hours, that kind of thing.'

I wondered aloud whether it would work, and the reply was, 'A crime is unlikely to be committed anywhere near one of these dogs.'

The Canine Squad is housed with a branch of the Mobile Task Force at the underground junction of the LL and GG lines; Lorimer Street–Metropolitan Avenue. The bulletin board on the plain-clothes men's side is plastered with unit citations and merit awards, and Sgt Donnery of the Task Force was recently made 'Cop of the Month' for a particularly clever set of arrests. Sgt Donnery is in charge of thirty-two plain-clothes men and two detectives. Their motto is 'Soar with the Eagles'. A sheaf of admiring newspaper clippings testifies to their effectiveness. As we talked, the second shift was preparing to set out for the day.

'Morale seems very high,' I said. The men were joking, watching, the old-man decoy spraying his hair and beard white.

'Sure, morale is high,' Sgt Donnery said. 'We feel we're getting something accomplished. It isn't easy. Sometimes you have to hide in a porter's room with a mop for four days before you get your man. We dress up as porters, conductors, motormen, track-workers. If there are a lot of robberies and track-workers in the same station, we dress up as track-workers. We've got all the uniforms.'

'Plain-clothes men' is something of a misnomer for the Task Force that has enough of a theatrical wardrobe to mount a production of Subways are for Sleeping.

And yet, looking at Howard Haag and Joseph Minucci standing on the platform at Nassau Avenue on the GG line, you would probably take them for a pair of physical-education teachers on the way to the school gym. They look tough, but not aggressively so; they are healthy and well-built – but some of that is padding: they both wear bullet-proof vests. Underneath the ordinary clothes the men are well armed. Each man carries a .38, a blackjack and a can of Mace. Minucci has a two-way radio.

Haag has been on the force for seventeen years, Minucci for almost seven. Neither has in that time ever fired his gun, though each has an excellent arrest record and a pride in detection. They are funny, alert and indefatigable, and together they make Starsky and Hutch look like a pair of hysterical cream-puffs.

Their job is also much harder than any City cop's. I had been told repeatedly that the average City cop would refuse to work in the conditions that the Transit Police endure every day. At Nassau Avenue, Minucci told me why.

'Look at the stations! They're dirty, they're cold, they're noisy. If you fire your gun you'll kill about ten innocent people – you're trapped here. You stand here some days and the cold and the dampness creep into your bones and you start shivering. And that smell – smell it? – it's like that all the time, and you've got to stand there and breathe it in. Bergen Street Station, the snow comes through the bars and you freeze. They call it "The Ice-Box". Then some days, kids recognise you – they've seen you make a collar – and they swear at you, call you names, try to get you to react, smoke pot right under your nose. "Here come the DT's" – that's what they call us. It's the conditions. They're awful. You have to take so much crap from these schoolkids. And your feet are killing you. So you sit down, read a newspaper, drink coffee, and then you get a rip from a shoofly –'

Minucci wasn't angry; he said all this in a smiling, ironical way. Like Howie Haag, he enjoys his work and takes it seriously. A 'shoofly', he explained, is a police inspector who rides the subway looking for officers who are goldbricking – though having a coffee on a cold day hardly seemed to me like goldbricking. 'We're not supposed to drink coffee,' Minucci said, and he went on to define other words in the Transit Police vocabulary: 'lushworker' (a person who robs drunks or sleeping passengers); and 'Flop Squad' (decoys who pretend to be asleep, in order to attract lushworkers).

Just then, as we were talking at Nassau, the station filled up with shouting boys – big ones, aged anywhere from fifteen to eighteen. There were hundreds of them and, with them, came the unmistakable odour of smouldering marijuana. They were boys from Automotive High School, heading south on the GG. They stood on the platform howling and screaming and sucking smoke out of their fingers, and when the train pulled in they began fighting towards the doors.

'You might see one of these kids being a pain in the neck, writing graffiti or smoking dope or something,' Howie Haag said. 'And you might wonder why we don't do anything. The reason is we're looking for something serious – robbers, snatchers, assault, stuff like that.'

Minucci said, 'The Vandalism Squad deals with window-kickers and graffiti. Normally we don't.'

Once on the train the crowd of yelling boys thinned out. I had seen this sort of activity before: boys get on the subway train and immediately bang through the connecting doors and walk from car to car. I asked Minucci why this was so.

'They're marking the people. See them? They're looking for an old lady near a door or something they can snatch, or a pocket they can pick. They're sizing up the situation. They're also heading for the last car. That's where they hang out on this train.'

Howie said, 'They want to see if we'll follow them. If we do, they'll mark us as cops.'

Minucci and Haag did not follow, though at each stop they took cautious looks out of the train, using the reflections in mirrors and windows.

'They play the doors when it's crowded,' Minucci said.

Howie said, 'School-kids can take over a train.'

'Look at that old lady,' Minucci said. 'She's doing everything wrong.'

The woman, in her late sixties, was sitting next to the door. Her wristwatch was exposed and her handbag dangled from the arm closest to the door. Minucci explained that one of the commonest subway crimes was inspired by this posture. The snatcher reached through the door from the platform and, just before the doors shut, he grabbed the bag or watch, or both; and then he was off, and the train was pulling out, with the victim trapped on board.

I wondered whether the plain-clothes men would warn her. They didn't. But they watched her closely, and when she got off they escorted her in an anonymous way. The old woman never knew how well protected she was and how any person making a move to rob her would have been hammered flat to the platform by the combined weight of Officers Minucci and Haag.

There were men on the train drinking wine out of bottles sheathed in paper bags. Such men are everywhere in New York, propped against walls, with bottle and bag. A few hours earlier, at Myrtle–Willoughby, I had counted forty-six men hanging around outside a housing project, drinking this way. I had found their idleness and their stares and their drunken slouching a little sinister.

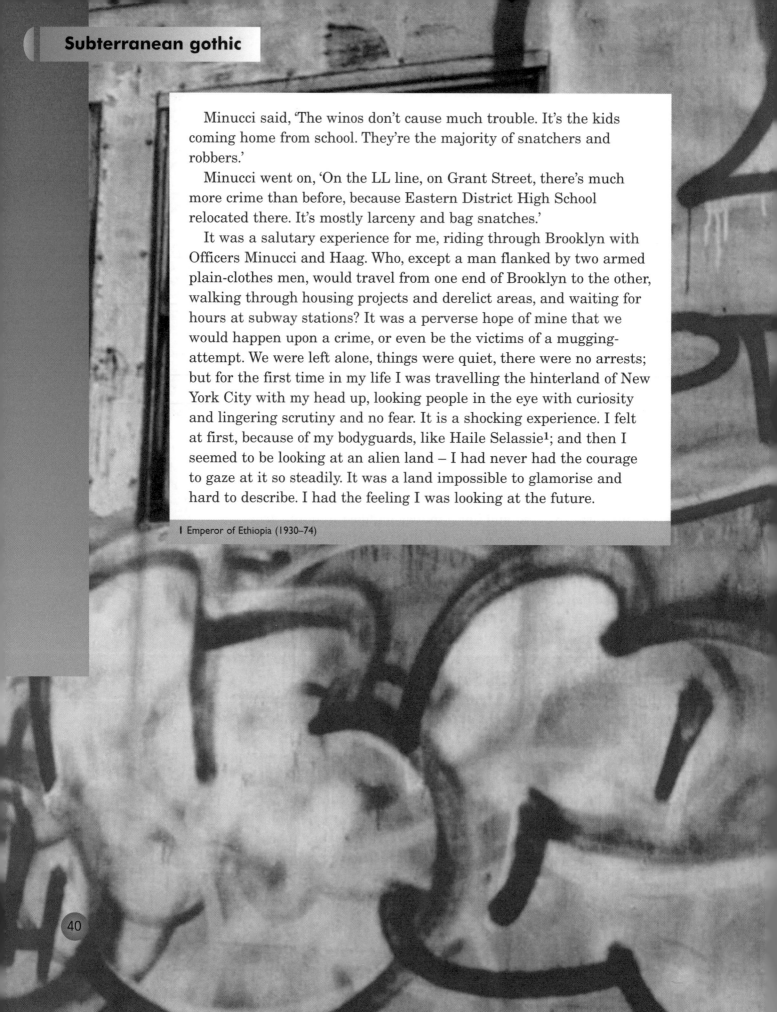

Minucci said, 'The winos don't cause much trouble. It's the kids coming home from school. They're the majority of snatchers and robbers.'

Minucci went on, 'On the LL line, on Grant Street, there's much more crime than before, because Eastern District High School relocated there. It's mostly larceny and bag snatches.'

It was a salutary experience for me, riding through Brooklyn with Officers Minucci and Haag. Who, except a man flanked by two armed plain-clothes men, would travel from one end of Brooklyn to the other, walking through housing projects and derelict areas, and waiting for hours at subway stations? It was a perverse hope of mine that we would happen upon a crime, or even be the victims of a mugging-attempt. We were left alone, things were quiet, there were no arrests; but for the first time in my life I was travelling the hinterland of New York City with my head up, looking people in the eye with curiosity and lingering scrutiny and no fear. It is a shocking experience. I felt at first, because of my bodyguards, like Haile Selassie[1]; and then I seemed to be looking at an alien land – I had never had the courage to gaze at it so steadily. It was a land impossible to glamorise and hard to describe. I had the feeling I was looking at the future.

1 Emperor of Ethiopia (1930–74)

Reading for meaning

1 The Transit Police have developed the strategy of using identifying headbands when they arrest a criminal at gunpoint. They use decoys dressed as helpless senior citizens. They wear bullet-proof vests. What does this tell you about the culture that exists in New York?

2 What factors make the job of the Transit cop a particularly hard one?

3 Why did Minucci and Haag choose not to warn the old lady on the train whose 'wristwatch was exposed and her handbag dangled from the arm closest to the door'?

4 What kind of experience did Paul Theroux have when he was 'riding through Brooklyn with Officers Minucci and Haag'? Why hadn't he felt like this before?

5 Why is 'Subterranean Gothic' an appropriate title for this piece of writing?

6 How does Paul Theroux structure this piece? Consider the way in which he has arranged the subject matter.

7 What punctuation devices does Paul Theroux use most frequently in his writing?

W 4b

Vocabulary and spelling

1 What is the link between the following words?

- disorientation
- misnomer
- incomprehensible
- indiscernible
- indefatigable

2 Find the meaning of 'disorientation' and 'misnomer'. What do the prefixes 'dis-' and 'mis-' mean?

3 Which of the following words take 'dis-' to make the antonym and which use 'mis-'?

- trust
- interest
- behave
- courteous
- print
- believe
- interpret
- entangle

Check your dictionary for the right answers. What is unusual about some of these words?

4 Find one-word definitions for the following words:

- manifest
- compliant
- advent
- citations
- salutary
- hinterland

5 Find some examples of slang and provide definitions.

Speaking and listening

The situation in the New York subways is obviously very serious and needs to improve. In groups of three, take on the roles of the following characters:

- NBC interviewer/reporter
- member of the public
- Mayor of New York.

Develop an interview for a prime-time news programme. The two interviewees should hold differing points of view.

Remember: It is important that the questions asked by the interviewer allow the guests to put forward their opinions. Avoid questions which can only be answered by 'yes' or 'no'.

Writing to inform, explain and describe

Reread the section of the text which describes an elderly lady sitting on the train, starting: '*Look at that old lady*,' on page 39, up to '*... out, with the victim trapped on board.*'

Write the report that Minucci or Haag might submit after making an arrest following a crime.

Sn 7

Writing to persuade, argue and advise

The New York subway has just undergone a facelift. The stations have been cleaned up and painted, there are more Transit Police on patrol and there is an efficient, computerised journey planning service.

Design an advertisement to encourage visitors and native New Yorkers to use the subway more. This advertisement will be placed on billboards, in magazines and newspapers, as well as on a flier to be distributed at bus stops and shopping malls.

Your design should use presentational devices such as: headings, bullets, text boxes, different fonts, colour and pictures.

Remember: You need to use the language as well as an attractive design to persuade your audience.

Writing to imagine, explore and entertain

Write your own 'gothic' description of an uncomfortable experience, real or imaginary, in which you detail what happened and how you felt.

Use the grid below to help plan your writing. Remember, the choice of vocabulary is incredibly important to the effect you achieve.

	Words/expressions	Intended effect
Where?		
Who?		
When?		
Sounds?		
What happened?		
How did the person respond?		

Review

With a partner, explore what you have learned in this chapter.

1 Choose:
- your best piece of work
- your least successful piece of work.

2 Read or allow your partner to read each piece of work. Explain to your partner the reasons for your choice. Identify features that you:
- used successfully
- need to develop.

Focus on Vocabulary and sentences

Individually, consider the following questions:

1 In this chapter, you have encountered interesting and varied vocabulary. What have you learned about the ways in which words are created?

2 Which five words will you try to remember? How will you remember them?

3 Select a paragraph of your own writing in which you use vocabulary well. What have you learned about the importance of using varied vocabulary? What could you improve in this paragraph?

4 What sentence punctuation techniques have you learned about in this section?

5 Give an example of three sentences in which you have used these techniques in your own writing. How well have you used them? What could you do to improve the sentences?

6 List five different techniques writers can use to create suspense.

7 In your own writing, find three examples where you have used these techniques. How successful was your attempt? What could you do to improve?

Based on your responses to these questions, set yourself up to three targets for improving your next piece of work. You might set targets such as:

a) experiment with different ways of learning spelling

b) include interesting vocabulary in my writing

c) use short, dramatic sentences in my writing.

Test Fact Box: The Reading paper

▶ You will be given a reading booklet and a question paper for this part of the test. The reading booklet contains three texts.

▶ The question paper will contain approximately 15 questions, about 5 on each text.

▶ You will need to answer all the questions.

▶ Each question is worth between 1 and 5 marks. The number of marks is an indication of how many points you need to make in your answer, but don't expect to get 1 mark for every comment!

▶ Each question has a specific assessment focus. There are five reading assessment focuses that are assessed:

Assessment focus 2: *describe, select or retrieve information, events or ideas from texts and use quotation and reference to the text.*

Assessment focus 3: *deduce, infer or interpret information, events or ideas from texts.*

Assessment focus 4: *comment on the structure and organisation of texts, including grammatical and presentational features at text level.*

Assessment focus 5: *comment on the writer's use of language, including grammatical and literary features at word and sentence level.*

Assessment focus 6: *identify and comment on writers' purposes and viewpoints, and the effect of the text on the reader.*

▶ Different question formats will be used on the reading paper: charts to complete; information to match or sequence; questions asking for words to be copied from the passage or explanations given in your own words; questions with several parts.

▶ Time allowed: 75 minutes.

The Reading test

Preparing for Assessment Focuses 2 and 3

Assessment Focus 2: describe, select or retrieve information, events or ideas from texts and use quotation and reference to the text.

This assessment focus asks you to find information in the text. Sometimes this can be explained in your own words and sometimes exact quotations are required. The questions will often ask you to 'find and copy' or 'list' evidence from the text.

Example

The following sample questions are based on The Eyes of the Poor. Reread the text on pages 24–25.

Paragraph three describes the decoration in the café. List five of the people illustrated on the walls. (2 marks)

1. Pages   **2.** Ladies   **3.** Nymphs   **4.** Goddesses   **5.** Hebe

Examiner's comments

There were six 'people' to choose from in the text: Pages, ladies, nymphs, goddesses, Hebe and Ganymede. The mark scheme allowed 1 mark for four correct answers, with the fifth correct response needed to gain the second mark. This response has correctly selected five and so gains the full 2 marks.

Practice

1 In the first paragraph, find and copy the narrator's criticism of his girlfriend. (1 mark)

2 In paragraph six, how did the narrator say he felt about being watched by the poor family? How did his girlfriend say she felt about them? (3 marks)

3 List two terms of endearment used by the narrator about his girlfriend in paragraphs six and seven. (2 marks)

4 In paragraph six, list two things that the narrator says the songs were right about. (2 marks)

Assessment Focus 3: deduce, infer or interpret information, events or ideas from texts.

This assessment focus asks you to work out the meaning of what you have read. You will need to 'read between the lines'. These questions often ask 'why' but might also ask you to 'find and copy' some information to support an inference, or 'explain' in order to interpret.

Example

How does the description of the café illustrate wealth? (4 marks)

The café is full of "sparkling" things that remind us of jewels. Everything either "shone" or "dazzled" which makes the café sound clean and expensive. It displays "splendour" which means that it must be really grand. Gold is also mentioned, which is a rich colour and associated with money. The bright light must have been expensive to maintain and makes us think the café has a lot of money. Also, it isn't a plain, cheap building – it has fancy decorations like "mouldings" and "cornices". The pictures are of rich people. There are "ladies" rather than "women". Only the rich would be able to afford "pages", or servants who are "chubby", suggesting that they are well fed. The ladies have falcons, which sound like special, unusual creatures. The "nymphs and the goddesses" give it a classical feel. The food that they are carrying is rich and plentiful. Fruit would have been expensive then and pâté is a delicacy. Game is expensive meat. It makes you think that you could eat these things in the café.

Examiner's comments

This is a full answer that picks out and comments on many different ideas in the paragraph. The connotations of the various colours and objects are explained and the meanings of words are explored. The explanations are clear and points are supported by concise references which are then explained further. Notice how the quotations are incorporated into the sentences. This response would have gained 4 marks.

Practice

1 Explain what paragraph five tells us about what each member of the family is thinking as they stare at the café. (3 marks)

2 Copy and explain two pieces of evidence to suggest that the family were poor (paragraph 4). (2 marks)

3 Why does the narrator say he hated his girlfriend, that their thoughts are 'incommunicable' and yet use terms of endearment like 'my love' and 'my angel'? (2 marks)

Test Fact Box: The Writing paper

▶ There is only one task on the writing paper.

▶ There are 30 marks available for the writing task.

▶ Your writing will be assessed for:
  - sentence structure and punctuation
  - text structure and organisation
  - composition and effect.

▶ Time allowed: 45 minutes including planning time.

The Writing test

Writing to inform, explain and describe

Example

The local council is reviewing public transport in your area in order to understand the strengths and weaknesses of the current services. It needs to decide how much should be spent improving public transport.

Write a formal report for your local council about the state of public transport in your area, recommending improvements that could be made. (30 marks)

Examiner's comments

*The main task is given in **bold** print and is introduced by some information that will help you to respond. In this example, you are told the **audience** for your writing (the local council), the **purpose** of the writing (to inform), the **type** of writing (a report), and the style of the writing (formal). You are also given some ideas about **content** (strengths and weaknesses of your local transport system, recommend improvements).*

Planning

Before you start writing your response, you should spend a few minutes noting down some key points and deciding how you will organise them. Good answers explore the issues in detail and are clearly organised.

Content

For your report you should:

- write an **opening paragraph** explaining the scope and focus of the report and making the structure of the report clear to the reader
- write a **concluding paragraph** that summarises the findings and indicates what happens next
- **explain** the **positive features** of the various forms of public transport in your area and the problems that exist. The problems could be in access to public transport, its efficiency, cost or safety
- **suggest** some **solutions** to the problems. These could be simple improvements in service or radical changes to the type of transport available. Make sure the benefits of these recommendations are clear.

Organisation and style

A report is an **information text.** You will need to use the features of this text type:

- *audience*: person/group involved in the content of the report (i.e. local council)
- *type of writing*: clear, factual, impersonal
- *text level*: information will be broken into sections, with headings
- *sentence level*: third person; present tense to describe how things are; active and passive voice; connectives to express sequence, cause and effect or comparison. Clarity is important in the sentence structure
- *word level*: precise vocabulary, including facts and figures. Meaning needs to be stated clearly rather than implied.

You could divide the report by form of transport (buses, trains, etc.) or by issues like comfort, convenience, cost, safety, etc. You could limit your report to particular aspects of public transport.

Here is part of a report written by a student in response to this task. Look at the features of report writing that have been used.

Buses

The bus service offered in Anytown is vital to many different groups of people. The service provides a cheap form of travel with a choice of three types of discounts available to regular users. Pensioners have a free off-peak bus pass that allows them to travel to visit relatives, go shopping and reach other leisure facilities. The bus stops are well placed for the shops and local businesses and all areas of the town are covered by bus routes. For this reason, they are well used during the rush-hour.

Examiner's comments

*There is a **sub-heading** ('Buses') that signals the content of this paragraph. The first sentence is the **topic sentence**, making a general point about the importance of buses. The paragraph then indicates the positive aspects of the bus service: cost and convenience. **Specific details** are given relating to each point. **Exact figures** are used ('choice of three') and the **vocabulary is precise** ('pensioners'). There are **different types of sentences** but they are clearly structured and link the ideas together. The connective 'For this reason' shows cause/effect.*

What might this student write about next? How might the report end?

Practice

Now write your own response to this task. As you write, remember to:
- use your plan
- choose vocabulary and sentence structures carefully
- keep in mind the reader of the report
- develop each point logically, adding appropriate detail
- compose in paragraphs and link the paragraphs
- read back what you have written to maintain consistency.

When you have finished, remember to check your work:
- Read it through to check it is logically organised and appropriately detailed.
- Read each sentence carefully, looking for technical errors. Tip: *Start with the final sentence and work your way back to the start, so you really do read each sentence separately and aren't tempted to jump forward in the text.*

② Visions of the future

We are all fascinated by the future: we read our horoscopes voraciously in the hope that they will tell us what to expect for our personal fortunes; we watch and read science fiction to be astounded by what our lives may become.

Writers have various visions for the future: bleak, terrifying futures where people destroy the world; ideal visions of how the world really should be and 'what if' scenarios – what if you won the lottery? What if women were only important in society if they could have children? This chapter looks at how the future has been imagined and how the future might be.

2.1 Utopias and dystopias

In this section you will encounter some writers who regard the future as a time when we could all live happily and everyone would be equal; they have a utopian vision. Other writers, who you will also meet in this section, predict the future to be a time of discontent and repression, or even imagine the world destroyed; theirs is a dystopian vision.

Utopia is an imaginary, perfect place. Thomas More, Henry VIII's chancellor, first used the term in his book called *Utopia*, which stated his vision for a better government in a better world. 'Utopia' is classical Greek for 'nowhere'.

The word **dystopia** was created to mean the opposite of Utopia: a world where all is wrong and unfair. The Greek prefix 'dys' means bad.

Imagine the Angels of Bread

'Imagine the Angels of Bread' is a political poem written about an imagined future. It was written by the American poet, Martin Espada in 1996.

Before you read

- List groups of people that you think could be placed in the category of those unfairly discriminated against, such as the homeless.

- Exchange your list with another student and write down who treats each group unfairly. For example: the homeless – employers; the homeless won't be given permanent employment without a permanent address.

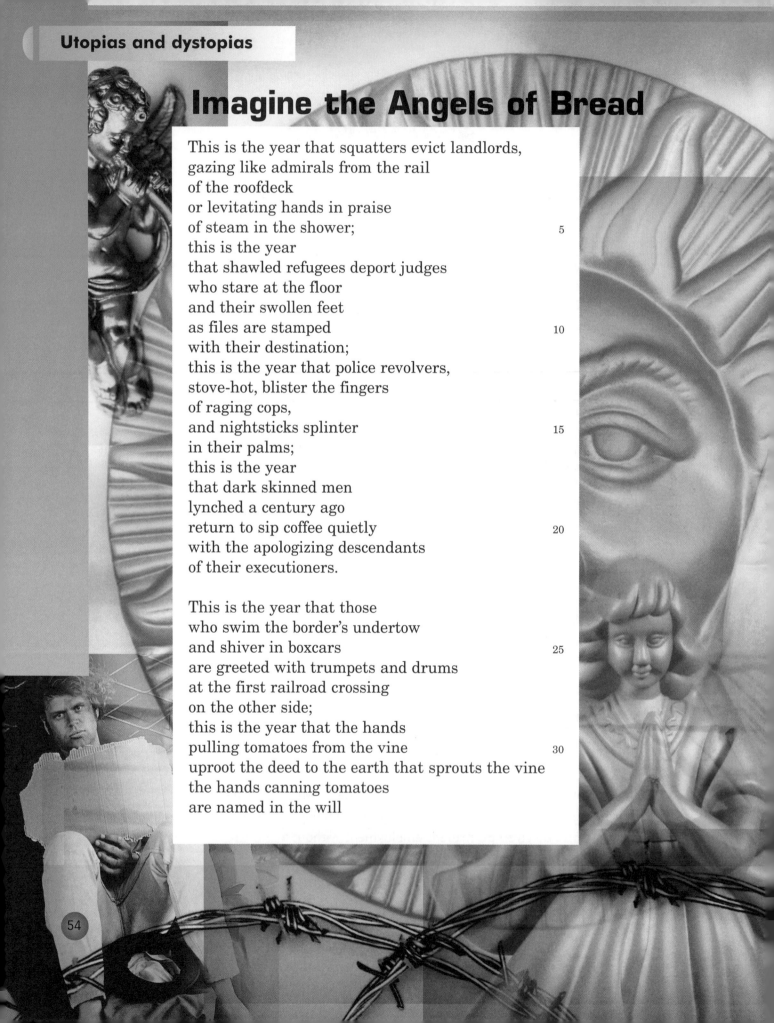

Imagine the Angels of Bread

This is the year that squatters evict landlords,
gazing like admirals from the rail
of the roofdeck
or levitating hands in praise
of steam in the shower;   5
this is the year
that shawled refugees deport judges
who stare at the floor
and their swollen feet
as files are stamped   10
with their destination;
this is the year that police revolvers,
stove-hot, blister the fingers
of raging cops,
and nightsticks splinter   15
in their palms;
this is the year
that dark skinned men
lynched a century ago
return to sip coffee quietly   20
with the apologizing descendants
of their executioners.

This is the year that those
who swim the border's undertow
and shiver in boxcars   25
are greeted with trumpets and drums
at the first railroad crossing
on the other side;
this is the year that the hands
pulling tomatoes from the vine   30
uproot the deed to the earth that sprouts the vine
the hands canning tomatoes
are named in the will

that owns the bedlam of the cannery;
this is the year that the eyes   35
stinging from the poison that purifies toilets
awaken at last to the sight
of a rooster-loud hillside,
pilgrimage of immigrant birth;
this is the year that cockroaches   40
become extinct, that no doctor
finds a roach embedded
in the ear of an infant;
this is the year that the food stamps
of adolescent mothers   45
are auctioned like gold doubloons,
and no coin is given to buy machetes
for the next bouquet of severed heads
in coffee plantation country.

If the abolition of slave-manacles   50
began as a vision of hands without manacles,
then this is the year;
if the shutdown of extermination camps
began as imagination of a land
without barbed wire or the crematorium,   55
then this is the year;
if every rebellion begins with the idea
that conquerors on horseback
are not many-legged gods, that they too drown
if plunged in the river,   60
then this is the year.

So may every humiliated mouth,
teeth like desecrated headstones,
fill with the angels of bread.

Martin Espada

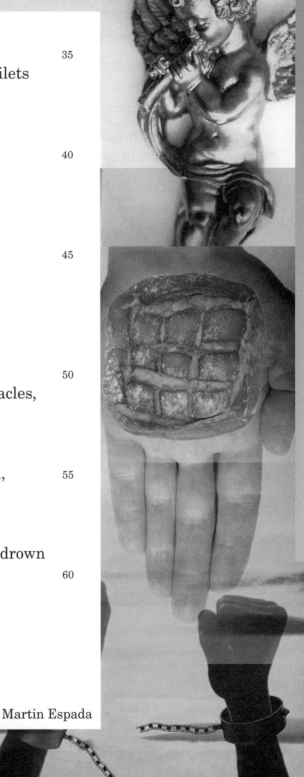

Reading for meaning

1 a) Identify all the groups in the poem that have suffered discrimination.

   b) What is the main reason for these groups being discriminated against? *Hint: African-American plantation slaves; Jewish internees of extermination camps?*

2 What happens to the victims of discrimination in this poem. Why is this unusual?

3 Consider the lines 57–60. What do you think the poet believes needs to happen before people can free themselves?
   Hint: If conquerors can drown, what is the poet trying to say about them and why would that help people to stand up against them?

4 a) Bread is a simple, staple food that everyone should have access to. What other images in the poem would you describe as ordinary?

   b) Angels are fanciful and fantastic creatures. Are there any other images in the poem that you would describe as fanciful and fantastic?

5 a) What is the poet saying about how change should be achieved?
   Hint: Should we wait for a miracle?

   b) Find examples in the poem to support your view.

W 7

Vocabulary

'This is the year that the eyes stinging from the poison that purifies toilets awaken at last ...'

a) Complete the spider diagram with other connotations suggested by the metaphor of the eyes that 'awaken'.

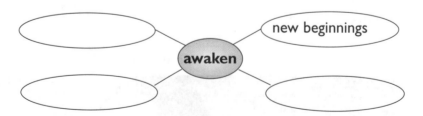

b) Find three more words or images in the poem with positive connotations and three words with negative connotations.

c) Use a thesaurus to find words that have similar meanings to the words you have selected. Substitute them for the words in the poem and comment on how the meaning changes.

Martin Espada's poetic technique

Rhetorical devices are writing techniques which are designed to have an impact upon the reader and cause them to react to what the writer has written. Martin Espada uses a number of these devices in his poem:

* **repetition** (using the same words/phrases more than once)

* **simile** (comparing two things, using the words 'like' or 'as')

* **juxtaposition** (placing words/ideas next to each other to make the reader think and question the text)

* **metaphor** (writing about something as if it were something else)

* **enjambement** (lines that don't end with a full stop, but run into the next line)

* **hypothesis** (introducing an idea with the word 'if', proposing 'what if we did this?')

* **persuasive language** (words/phrases which attempt to make you accept the writer's opinion)

1 Find an example of each of the rhetorical devices used by Martin Espada in his poem and describe the effect it has upon you as a reader.

2 a) How is the poem structured? Divide it into sections that relate to units of meaning.

b) How could you describe this structure? *Hint: Where might you use this structure in which the facts are presented first, the ideas about what could be done are given second, and the point of your argument is given at the end?*

Do Androids Dream of Electric Sheep?

This extract in this section is taken from the science-fiction novel *Do Androids Dream of Electric Sheep?* by the American writer Philip K. Dick. This is the book that inspired the film *Blade Runner*. In this section from the novel opening, we meet the central character, Rick Deckard, and his wife, Iran. Deckard is a bounty hunter who seeks and kills androids for a living.

Before you read

- In pairs, discuss what technological advances there have been in the last fifty years.
- What advances in technology do you think will take place in the next fifty years?

Vocabulary

W 7

1 a) The term 'android' is used to refer to a type of being in this novel. What does this term mean?

   b) What is the origin of the word? Use a dictionary to help you.

2 What is a 'bounty hunter'? What are the connotations attached to this particular profession?

3 Why do you think that the existence of andriods might be threatening to human beings?

Do Androids Dream of Electric Sheep?

A merry little surge of electricity piped by automatic alarm from the mood organ beside his bed awakened Rick Deckard. Surprised – it always surprised him to find himself awake without prior notice – he rose from the bed, stood up in his multicolored pajamas, and stretched. Now, in her bed, his wife Iran opened her gray, unmerry eyes, blinked, then groaned and shut her eyes again.

'You set your Penfield too weak,' he said to her. 'I'll reset it and you'll be awake and – '

'Keep your hand off my settings.' Her voice held bitter sharpness. 'I don't want to be awake.'

He seated himself beside her, bent over her, and explained softly. 'If you set the surge up high enough, you'll be glad you're awake; that's the whole point. At setting C it overcomes the threshold barring consciousness, as it does for me.' Friendlily, because he felt well-disposed toward the world – his setting had been at D – he patted her bare, pale shoulder.

'Get your crude cop's hand away,' Iran said.

'I'm not a cop.' He felt irritable now, although he hadn't dialed for it.

'You're worse,' his wife said, her eyes still shut. 'You're a murderer hired by the cops.'

'I've never killed a human being in my life.' His irritability had risen, now; had become outright hostility.

Iran said, 'Just those poor andys.'

'I notice you've never had any hesitation as to spending the bounty money I bring home on whatever momentarily attracts your attention.' He rose, strode to the console of his mood organ. 'Instead of saving,' he said, 'so we could buy a real sheep, to replace that fake electric one upstairs. A mere electric animal, and me earning all that I've worked my way up to through the years.' At his console he hesitated between dialing for a thalamic suppressant (which would abolish his mood rage) or a thalamic stimulant (which would make him irked enough to win the argument).

'If you dial,' Iran said, eyes open and watching, 'for greater venom, then I'll dial the same. I'll dial the maximum and you'll see a fight that makes every argument we've had up to now seem like nothing. Dial and see; just try me.' She rose swiftly, loped to the console of her own mood organ, stood glaring at him, waiting.

He sighed, defeated by her threat. 'I'll dial what's on my schedule for today.' Examining the schedule for January 3, 1992, he saw that a businesslike professional attitude was called for. 'If I dial by a schedule,' he said warily, 'will you agree to also?' He waited, canny enough not to commit himself until his wife had agreed to follow suit.

'My schedule for today lists a six-hour self-accusatory depression,' Iran said.

'What? Why did you schedule that?' It defeated the whole purpose of the mood organ. 'I didn't know you could set it for that,' he said gloomily.

'I was sitting here one afternoon,' Iran said, 'and naturally I turned on Buster Friendly and His Friendly Friends and he was talking about a big news item he's about to break and then that awful commercial came on, the one I hate; you know, for Mountibank Lead Codpieces. And so for a minute I shut off the sound. And I hear the building, this building; I heard the –' She gestured.

'Empty apartments,' Rick said. Sometimes he heard them at night when he was supposed to be asleep. And yet, for this day and age a one-half occupied conapt building rated high in the scheme of population density; out in what had been before the war the suburbs one could find buildings entirely empty … or so he had heard. He had let the information remain secondhand; like most people he did not care to experience it directly.

'At that moment,' Iran said, 'when I had the TV sound off, I was in a 382 mood; I had just dialed it. So although I heard the emptiness intellectually, I didn't feel it. My first reaction consisted of being grateful that we could afford a Penfield mood organ. But then I realized how unhealthy it was, sensing the absence of life, not just in this building but everywhere, and not reacting – do you see? I guess you don't. But that used to be considered a sign of mental illness; they called it 'absence of appropriate effect.' So I left the TV sound off and I sat down at my mood organ and I experimented. And I finally found a setting for despair' Her dark, pert face showed satisfaction, as if she had achieved something of worth. 'So I put it on my schedule for twice a month; I think that's a reasonable amount of time to feel hopeless about everything, about staying here on Earth after everybody who's smart has emigrated, don't you think?'

Reading for meaning

1 What is the Penfield machine and what purpose does it have? How does it operate?

2 What do we learn about the relationship between Deckard and his wife?

3 Deckard mentions buying '*a real sheep, to replace that fake electric one upstairs*'. What does this suggest about the world in which they live?

4 The author has set this story in 1992. How does the world the Deckards live in differ from our world of today? What might have caused these changes?

5 At the end of this extract, Iran says that 'everybody who's smart has emigrated'. Why do think they have emigrated? Where have they emigrated to?

Drama

1 Work in pairs to focus on the relationship between Deckard and Iran. One of you should take the character of Deckard and the other Iran. Make bullet points to track what you learn about each character and their relationship.

2 Role-play the conversation that might have taken place if Deckard had chosen to use a thalamic stimulant. (You may need to investigate the meaning of this term beforehand.)

3 In pairs discuss to what extent you think Deckard and his wife behave like 'natural' human beings. Can you think of anything that we use to affect moods as in this extract?

Writing to imagine, explore and entertain

Design an advertisement for the latest model of the Penfield mood organ. In your advertisement you should include information on:

- new features

- how it operates

- what effect it has

- what it looks like.

Remember that the purpose of this advertisement is to persuade the target audience to purchase a Penfield mood organ.

Wr 14

Writing to persuade, argue and advise

1 In this conversation between Deckard and his wife, we learn about their respective attitudes to 'andys'. What are their attitudes?

'You're worse,' his wife said, her eyes still shut. 'You're a murderer hired by the cops.'
'I've never killed a human being in my life.' His irritability had risen, now; had become outright hostility.
Iran said, 'Just those poor andys.'

2 a) Now, write three paragraphs in which you argue as Iran, persuading Deckard that 'those poor andys' deserve the same opportunities and rights as humans.

b) How do you think Deckard would respond?

In this next extract, Deckard is visiting the large corporation that manufactured the androids he is hunting. The technology used in creating the androids is so advanced that they appear and behave exactly like humans. He is trying to find out if the Voigt-Kampff test he uses will be able to recognise a new sophisticated type of android, the Nexus 6. He doesn't know if Rachael is an android.

It, he thought. She keeps calling the owl it. Not her. 'Just a second,' he said.

Pausing at the door, Rachael said, 'You've decided?'

'I want,' he said, opening his briefcase, 'to ask you one more question from the Voigt-Kampff scale. Sit down again.'

Rachael glanced at her uncle; he nodded and she grudgingly returned, seating herself as before. 'What's this for?' she demanded, her eyebrows lifted in distaste – and wariness. He perceived her skeletal tension, noted it professionally.

Presently he had the pencil of light trained on her right eye and the adhesive patch again in contact with her cheek. Rachael stared into the light rigidly, the expression of extreme distaste still manifest.

'My briefcase,' Rick said as he rummaged for the Voigt-Kampff forms. 'Nice, isn't it? Department issue.'

'Well, well,' Rachael said remotely.

'Babyhide,' Rick said. He stroked the black leather surface of the briefcase. 'One hundred per cent genuine human baby- hide.' He saw the two dial indicators gyrate frantically. But only after a pause. The reaction had come, but too late. He knew the reaction period down to a fraction of a second, the correct reaction period; there should have been none. 'Thanks, Miss Rosen,' he said, and gathered together the equipment again; he had concluded his retesting. 'That's all.'

'You're leaving?' Rachael asked.

'Yes,' he said. 'I'm satisfied.'

Cautiously, Rachael said, 'What about the other nine subjects?'

'The scale has been adequate in your case,' he answered. 'I can extrapolate from that; it's clearly still effective.' To Eldon Rosen, who slumped morosely by the door of the room, he said, 'Does she know?' Sometimes they didn't; false memories had been tried various times, generally in the mistaken idea that through them reactions to testing would be altered.

Eldon Rosen said, "No. We programmed her completely. But I think toward the end she suspected." To the girl he said, "You guessed when he asked for one more try."

Pale, Rachael nodded fixedly.

Reading for meaning

1 What is the purpose of Deckard's visit to the Rosen Corporation?

2 At the start of the extract, what do we understand the relationship between Rachael and Eldon Rosen to be? How does this change by the end of the extract?

3 When Deckard calls Rachael back, how does she respond? Why does she respond in this way?

4 How does the Voigt-Kampff test work? List the steps Deckard takes when he sets up the test.

5 a) What are Deckard's conclusions about Rachael after he administers the test?

   b) What reasons does Deckard have for reaching this conclusion?

   c) What does the test tell you about what the definition of a human being is?

6 Consider both extracts again. Compare the ways in which the author represents humans (in Deckard and Iran) and androids. What are you supposed to feel about these characters? How does Philip K. Dick create that response?

Sentences, punctuation and vocabulary

1 Look again at the opening two lines of this extract. What do you notice that is unusual about the way in which the author has written these two lines? What effect is created by using this technique?

2 Consider the two extracts carefully. What would you say were the characteristics of Philip K. Dick's narrative style? Think about:

   • sentence types and lengths, and how they are punctuated

   • use of dialogue

   • specialist science fiction vocabulary.

3 Now, using these same stylistic features, write the next two paragraphs of the chapter. You should start your paragraphs with:

'Pale, Rachael nodded fixedly.'

Speaking and listening

'Fiction has been predicting it for years, but now reality shows our world is heading for disaster, both environmentally and culturally.'

In light of your experience of the texts studied in this chapter and your knowledge of current affairs, discuss this statement in a formal debate. You should:

- appoint a chairperson to manage the discussion

- have two people who support the statement

- have two people who oppose the statement

- encourage everyone in the group to think about their opinions.

At the end of the debate, agree an action plan outlining what could be done to help protect our world from the futures we have seen, read and talked about.

Writing to compare

Compare the way in which minority groups are represented in Martin Espada's poem and the Philip K. Dick novel. You should write three paragraphs covering the following points:

- Who the minority groups are and how they are treated by the society in which they exist

- How the author represents the minority groups

- What the reader's response to these groups is.

The Handmaid's Tale

The Handmaid's Tale is a novel written by Margaret Atwood, a Canadian author. It presents a dystopian vision of a society governed by men. The country is called Gilead, but was formerly known as the USA. The government rules through fear and oppression: all forms of communication have been banned and, because of the fall in the birthrate of white children, women are now only significant if they can bear children. Older single women, homosexual men and those who cannot have children are sent to the colonies to clear up toxic spills. The novel itself focuses on a character called Offred who is forced to serve as a surrogate mother and is made to give up her own child and husband in order to do this.

The Handmaid's Tale
Chapter Two

A chair, a table, a lamp. Above, on the white ceiling, a relief ornament in the shape of a wreath, and in the centre of it a blank space, plastered over, like the place in a face where the eye has been taken out. There must have been a chandelier, once. They've removed anything you could tie a rope to.

A window, two white curtains. Under the window, a window seat with a little cushion. When the window is partly open – it only opens partly – the air can come in and make the curtains move. I can sit in the chair, or on the window seat, hands folded, and watch this. Sunlight comes in through the window too, and falls on the floor, which is made of wood, in narrow strips, highly polished. I can smell the polish. There's a rug on the floor, oval, of braided rags. This is the kind of touch they like: folk art, archaic, made by women, in their spare time, from things that have no further use. A return to traditional values. Waste not want not. I am not being wasted. Why do I want?

On the wall above the chair, a picture, framed but with no glass: a print of flowers, blue irises, watercolour. Flowers are still allowed. Does each of us have the same print, the same chair, the same white curtains, I wonder? Government issue?

Think of it as being in the army, said Aunt Lydia.

A bed. Single, mattress medium-hard, covered with a flocked white spread. Nothing takes place in the bed but sleep; or no sleep. I try not to think too much. Like other things now, thought must be rationed. There's a lot that doesn't bear thinking about. Thinking can hurt your chances, and I intend to last. I know why there is no glass in front of the watercolour picture of blue irises, and why the window only opens partly and why the glass in it is shatterproof. It isn't running away they're afraid of. We wouldn't get far. It's those other escapes, the ones you can open in yourself, given a cutting edge.

So. Apart from these details, this could be a college guest room, for the less distinguished visitors; or a room in a rooming house, of former times, for ladies in reduced circumstances. That is what we are now. The circumstances have been reduced; for those of us who still have circumstances.

But a chair, sunlight, flowers: these are not to be dismissed. I am alive, I live, I breathe, I put my hand out, unfolded, into the sunlight. Where I am is not a prison but a privilege, as Aunt Lydia said, who was in love with either/or.

The bell that measures time is ringing. Time here is measured by bells, as once in nunneries. As in a nunnery too, there are few mirrors.

I get up out of the chair, advance my feet into the sunlight, in their red shoes, flat-heeled to save the spine and not for dancing. The red gloves are lying on the bed. I pick them up, pull them onto my hands, finger by finger. Everything except the wings around my face is red: the colour of blood, which defines us. The skirt is ankle-length, full, gathered to a flat yoke that extends over the breasts, the sleeves are full. The white wings too are prescribed issue, they are to keep us from seeing, but also from being seen. I never looked good in red, it's not my colour. I pick up the shopping basket, put it over my arm.

The door of the room – not my room, I refuse to say my – is not locked. In fact it doesn't shut properly. I go out into the polished hallway, which has a runner down the centre, dusty pink. Like a path through the forest, like a carpet for royalty, it shows me the way.

The carpet bends and goes down the front staircase and I go with it, one hand on the banister, once a tree, turned in another century, rubbed to a warm gloss. Late Victorian, the house is a family house, built for a large rich family. There's a grandfather clock in the hallway, which doles out time, and then the door to the motherly front sitting room, with its fleshtones and hints. A sitting room in which I never sit, but stand or kneel only. At the end of the hallway, above the front door, is a fanlight of coloured glass: flowers, red and blue.

There remains a mirror, on the hall wall. If I turn my head so that the white wings framing my face direct my vision towards it, I can see it as I go down the stairs, round, convex, a pier-glass, like the eye of a fish, and myself in it like a distorted shadow, a parody of something, some fairytale figure in a red cloak, descending towards a moment of carelessness that is the same as danger. A Sister, dipped in blood.

At the bottom of the stairs there's a hat-and-umbrella stand, the bentwood kind, long rounded rungs of wood curving gently up into hooks shaped like the opening fronds of a fern. There are several umbrellas in it: black, for the Commander, blue, for the Commander's Wife, and the one assigned to me, which is red. I leave the red umbrella where it is, because I know from the window that the day is sunny. I wonder whether or not the Commander's Wife is in the sitting room. She doesn't always sit. Sometimes I can hear her pacing back and forth, a heavy step and then a light one, and the soft tap of her cane on the dusty-rose carpet.

I walk along the hallway, past the sitting-room door and the door that leads into the dining room, and open the door at the end of the hall and go through into the kitchen. Here the smell is no longer of furniture polish. Rita is in here, standing at the kitchen table, which has a top of chipped white enamel. She's in her usual Martha's dress, which is dull green, like a surgeon's gown of the time before. The dress is much like mine in shape, long and concealing, but with a bib apron over it and without the white wings and the veil. She puts the veil on to go outside, but nobody much cares who sees the face of a Martha. Her sleeves are rolled to the elbow, showing her brown arms. She's making bread, throwing the loaves for the final brief kneading and then the shaping.

Rita sees me and nods, whether in greeting or in simple acknowledgement of my presence it's hard to say, and wipes her floury hands on her apron and rummages in the kitchen drawer for the token book. Frowning, she tears out three tokens and hands them to me. Her face might be kindly if she would smile. But the frown isn't personal: it's the red dress she disapproves of, and what it stands for. She thinks I may be catching, like a disease or any form of bad luck.

Sometimes I listen outside closed doors, a thing I never would have done in the time before. I don't listen long, because I don't want to be caught doing it. Once, though, I heard Rita say to Cora that she wouldn't debase herself like that.

Nobody asking you, Cora said. Anyways, what could you do, supposing?

Go to the Colonies, Rita said. They have the choice.

With the Unwomen, and starve to death and Lord knows what all? said Cora. Catch you.

They were shelling peas; even through the almost-closed door I could hear the light clink of the hard peas falling into the metal bowl. I heard Rita, a grunt or a sigh, of protest or agreement.

Anyways, they're doing it for us all, said Cora, or so they say. If I hadn't of got my tubes tied, it could of been me, say I was ten years younger. It's not that bad. It's not what you'd call hard work.

Better her than me, Rita said, and I opened the door. Their faces were the way women's faces are when they've been talking about you behind your back and they think you've heard: embarrassed, but also a little defiant, as if it were their right. That day, Cora was more pleasant to me than usual, Rita more surly.

Today, despite Rita's closed face and pressed lips, I would like to stay here, in the kitchen. Cora might come in, from somewhere else in the house, carrying her bottle of lemon oil and her duster, and Rita would make coffee – in the houses of the Commanders there is still real coffee – and we would sit at Rita's kitchen table, which is not Rita's any more than my table is mine, and we would talk, about aches and pains, illnesses, our feet, our backs, all the different kinds of mischief that our bodies, like unruly children, can get up to. We would nod our heads as punctuation to each other's voices, signalling that yes, we know all about it. We would exchange remedies and try to outdo each other in the recital of our physical miseries; gently we would complain, our voices soft and minor-key and mournful as pigeons in the eaves troughs. *I know what you mean*, we'd say. Or, a quaint expression you sometimes hear, still, from older people: *I hear where you're coming from*, as if the voice itself were a traveller, arriving from a distant place. Which it would be, which it is.

How I used to despise such talk. Now I long for it. At least it was talk. An exchange, of sorts.

Or we would gossip. The Marthas know things, they talk among themselves, passing the unofficial news from house to house. Like me, they listen at doors, no doubt, and see things even with their eyes averted. I've heard them at it sometimes, caught whiffs of their private conversations. *Stillborn, it was.* Or, *Stabbed her with a knitting needle, right in the belly. Jealousy, it must have been, eating her up.* Or, tantalizingly, *It was toilet cleaner she used. Worked like a charm, though you'd think he'd of tasted it. Must've been that drunk; but they found her out all right.*

Or I would help Rita to make the bread, sinking my hands into that soft resistant warmth which is so much like flesh. I hunger to touch something, other than cloth or wood. I hunger to commit the act of touch.

But even if I were to ask, even if I were to violate decorum to that extent, Rita would not allow it. She would be too afraid. The Marthas are not supposed to fraternize with us.

Fraternize means *to behave like a brother.* Luke told me that. He said there was no corresponding word that meant to *behave like a sister. Sororize*, it would have to be, he said. From the Latin. He liked knowing about such details. The derivations of words, curious usages. I used to tease him about being pedantic.

I take the tokens from Rita's outstretched hand. They have pictures on them, of the things they can be exchanged for: twelve eggs, a piece of cheese, a brown thing that's supposed to be a steak. I place them in the zippered pocket in my sleeve, where I keep my pass.

"Tell them fresh, for the eggs," she says. "Not like the last time. And a chicken, tell them, not a hen. Tell them who it's for and then they won't mess around."

"All right," I say. I don't smile. Why tempt her to friendship?

Reading for meaning

1 a) Identify the different ranks of people in the extract.

   b) Which colour is associated with each rank? What are the
      connotations of each colour?

2 How is Offred regarded by other ranks in this society? Give evidence
   for your view.

3 Comment on the appearance of Offred's room. Why have objects
   been removed from it?

4 Can we tell anything about Offred's personality from the following
   quotation: 'Thinking can hurt your chances, and I intend to last.'?

5 Offred is given tokens to exchange for food; the tokens have no
   words written on them, only pictures. Why do you think this might
   be? *Hint: Why would the written word be threatening to the government of
   Gilead?*

6 Comment on the effect of the opening sentences of the first three
   paragraphs.

   • Are they grammatically complete?

   • How do they contribute to the mood of the extract?

7 a) Why do you think the author puts the overheard conversations in
      italics and writes them in such short sentences: '*Stillborn, it was*'?

   b) What effect does this have in the midst of Offred's first person
      account?

8 What do we know about the way the women treat one another in
   Gilead from this extract? *Hint: Look at all the mentions of women that
   Offred makes. Do you notice anything?*

Vocabulary

W 7

1 Why do you think Offred refuses to describe the room as *'my* room' and refers to it as *'the* room'?

2 The women who cannot have children and serve no other 'productive' purpose are sent to the Colonies. They are referred to as 'Unwomen'. Describe the effect of this word.

3 Offred tells us that there is no female equivalent for the word *'fraternize … to behave like a brother'*. What is Atwood saying about a society which doesn't have such a word?

Speaking and listening

Work in threes, two of you in role as Offred and her male employer, and one observer.

- Offred and her male employer each give a two-minute presentation on what is right or wrong about the role of woman in Gilead society.

- The observer listens to the arguments, and concludes by stating which argument they feel was the more convincing and why.

Writing to imagine, explore and entertain

Wr 5

Rita, one of the characters in this extract, is a 'Martha' in Gilead society. In the Bible, Martha was a busy, practical character who cooked and provided for Jesus. Reread from page 69 to the end of the extract.

- Write notes on what you think a Martha's role is in this society, and what the extract tells us her attitude would be to Handmaids like Offred and towards the commander and his wife.

- Write an account of a day from Rita's perspective. You might want to start your account in Rita's room first thing in the morning.

2.2   The end of the world

The greatest fear most of us have is death, as it is the one thing over which we have no control. Attendant to this fear, is a collective paranoia about the end of the world. In the twentieth century there were two world wars; nuclear weapons that could lead to mass destruction were developed; and the danger of global warming and environmental collapse was always present. Throughout time there have been threats of war, famine and plague. Cultures have responded to these fears by developing stories and end-of-the-world scenarios.

Speaking and listening

What end-of-the-world stories have you heard or read, perhaps on the television or related to religion or another culture?

The Second Coming

Christians believe that after a second coming Christ will establish heaven on earth. W. B. Yeats's poem is written in denial of that hope, for he predicts that at the end of the millennium there will arise not Christ but the anti-christ: a savage god whose reign will be tyrannical and certainly not a heaven on earth.

The poem was written in direct response to the First World War (1914–18). Yeats wrote the poem in January 1919 when the world was still coming to terms with the horrific consequences of what was meant to be the war to end all wars. The war against Germany resulted in a huge loss of life, with a generation of young men being destroyed by the brutalities of trench warfare. The poem shows Yeats's despair at what he saw of humanity.

The Second Coming

Turning and turning in the widening gyre

The falcon cannot hear the falconer;

Things fall apart; the centre cannot hold;

Mere anarchy is loosed upon the world,

The blood-dimmed tide is loosed, and everywhere   5

The ceremony of innocence is drowned;

The best lack all conviction, while the worst

Are full of passionate intensity.

Surely some revelation is at hand;

Surely the Second Coming is at hand.   10

The Second Coming! Hardly are those words out

When a vast image out of Spiritus Mundi

Troubles my sight: somewhere in sands of the desert

A shape with lion body and the head of a man,

A gaze blank and pitiless as the sun,   15

Is moving its slow thighs, while all about it

Reel shadows of the indignant desert birds.

The darkness drops again; but now I know

That twenty centuries of stony sleep

Were vexed to nightmare by a rocking cradle,   20

And what rough beast, its hour come round at last,

Slouches towards Bethlehem to be born?

W. B. Yeats

Reading for meaning

W 7

1 Write down words and phrases from the poem that show the world is falling apart or is not functioning as it should.

2 Yeats writes: '*The falcon cannot hear the falconer*' (line 2).

   a) A falcon is a bird of prey, the falconer its handler. If the falcon couldn't hear its handler what would be the problem?

   b) If we (as humans) are the falcon, who might be the falconer?

   c) If the humans cannot hear their equivalent of the falconer, what sort of problems would this cause in the world?

3 Why do lines 7–8 suggest that there is no hope?

   • Who might 'the best' be and why might they now lack belief?

   • After the war who might be considered to be 'the worst' and why might they be full of enthusiasm? What would this enthusiasm be for?

4 The word 'surely' starts the second section. This section is about the state of the world at the time Yeats was writing.

   a) Summarise the subject of the second section.

   b) How does the form of the poem reflect the poem's meaning?

   c) Comment on the effect of the repetition of 'surely'.

5 a) The image of the '*shape with lion body and the head of a man*' (line 14) resembles the sphinx. Yeats changes the image slightly by making the beast male. Research the sphinx of Greek mythology.

   b) Why does Yeats make reference to this particular legend?

6 Why do you think Yeats has written the poem in blank verse?
   Hint: Would an ordered rhyme scheme have suited the topic of the poem?

Blank verse is when poetry has a regular rhythm or metre, but no rhyme. The writer may vary the number of beats per line, and the sequence of stressed and unstressed beats, to give a particular emphasis or effect.

In this poem Edwin Muir (1887–1959), like Yeats, is writing about his vision of the end of the world; for him the aftermath of a nuclear war.

The Horses

Barely a twelvemonth after
The seven days war that put the world to sleep,
Late in the evening the strange horses came.
By then we had made our covenant with silence,
But in the first few days it was so still   5
We listened to our breathing and were afraid.
On the second day
The radios failed; we turned the knobs; no answer.
On the third day a warship passed us, heading north,
Dead bodies piled on the deck. On the sixth day   10
A plane plunged over us into the sea. Thereafter
Nothing. The radios dumb;
And still they stand in corners of our kitchens,
And stand, perhaps, turned on, in a million rooms
All over the world. But now if they should speak,   15
If on a sudden they should speak again,
If on the stroke of noon a voice should speak,
We would not listen, we would not let it bring
That old bad world that swallowed its children quick
At one great gulp. We would not have it again.   20
Sometimes we think of the nations lying asleep,
Curled blindly in impenetrable sorrow,
And then the thought confounds us with its strangeness.
The tractors lie about our fields; at evening
They look like dank sea-monsters couched and waiting.   25
We leave them were they are and let them rust:
'They'll moulder away and be like other loam'.
We make our oxen drag our rusty ploughs,
Long laid aside. We have gone back
Far past our fathers' land.   30
        And then, that evening
Late in the summer the strange horses came.
We heard a distant tapping on the road,

A deepening drumming; it stopped, went on again
And at the corner changed to hollow thunder.   35
We saw the heads
Like a wild wave charging and were afraid.
We had sold our horses in our fathers' time
To buy new tractors. Now they were strange to us
As fabulous steeds set on an ancient shield   40
Or illustrations in a book of knights.
We did not dare go near them. Yet they waited,
Stubborn and shy, as if they had been sent
By an old command to find our whereabouts
And that long-lost archaic companionship.   45
In the first moment we had never a thought
That they were creatures to be owned and used.
Among them were some half a dozen colts
Dropped in some wilderness of the broken world,
Yet new as if they had come from their own Eden.   50
Since then they have pulled our ploughs and borne our loads
But that free servitude still can pierce our hearts.
Our life is changed; their coming our beginning.

Edwin Muir

Reading for meaning

1 How long has it been since the nuclear attack?

2 What do lines 4–6 show us about how the people were affected by the attack? *Hint: Do their reactions change over time?*

3 All modern civilisation has gone: even the radios are useless, yet the people keep them switched on. Why do you think this is?

4 What state is the world in if it has '*gone back/Far past our fathers' land*' (lines 29–30)?

5 What does line 52 tell us about how the people feel towards the horses?

6 How will the horses help to save the people?

Speaking and listening

Muir's vision of the post-nuclear world seems to be a utopian one. What criticisms is Muir making of our society and values through this utopian vision?

Comparative reading for meaning

1 a) Yeats's poem 'The Second Coming' begins with an observational style then adopts the first-person in the second stanza. What is the effect of this?

   b) However, in 'The Horses', Muir repeatedly uses the pronoun 'we'. What effect does this have on the reader of Muir's poem?

2 a) Muir refers to the '… seven days war that put the world to sleep' (line 2). What biblical event is supposed to have taken place over seven days?

   b) Why might Muir choose to make this allusion?

   c) Both Yeats and Muir refer to religion, either directly or indirectly. Why would they include such references when writing about the end of the world?

3 Both Muir and Yeats divided their poems into two sections.

   a) For each poem, summarise briefly what both sections are about.

   b) Yeats connected both sections through echoing 'surely'. How does Muir link his two sections?

4 Yeats's poem ends with a question, emphasising the uncertainty that Yeats feels for the future of the world. How is Muir's ending different and what is it about the structure of his final sentence that makes it so much more definite?

Writing to analyse, review and comment

Yeats and Muir both write about their vision for the end of the world. Which vision is more effective and why?

This question is asking you to compare how different poets write about a similar subject. You need to think about the following things:

- **content** (what the poems are actually about, their subject matter)

- **voice** (who is speaking the poem and how they are speaking)

- **form** (what type of poem is it? How is it written – does it rhyme, for instance?)

- **purpose** (what reason do you think the poet had for writing?)

- **evaluation** (considering all of the above, which of the two poems do you think works better)

Plan your answer as follows:

- Write at least one paragraph for each section and use quotations from the text to support the points you make.

- Plan your answer so each paragraph is comparative.

- Take 30 minutes to write up your answer. Write in standard English and leave five minutes to check your spelling and punctuation.

2.3 Personal happiness

Utopian and dystopian visions of the future often focus on global events and global predictions. However, for most of us, considering the future is a much more personal experience: we dream, perhaps, of winning the lottery and having the perfect life, free from worry or effort. The following extracts consider this notion of the future on a personal level and the lengths people might go to in order to attain their own future happiness.

Freedom Ship

This article from *The Observer* concerns a ship built to offer an alternative form of housing. The ship will sail the world's oceans, have all its own facilities and have expensive accommodation for 40,000 people.

Before you read

- What do you think would attract someone to live on a huge ship that moves around the world?

- Would you like to live on such a ship? Explain your answer.

Freedom Ship 'target for terrorists'

Jason Burke

It has been billed as a maritime Utopia sailing the seven seas. But security experts are warning that the 40,000 people who are expected to buy homes on the mile-long, 300-yard wide Freedom Ship may find life closer to *Blade Runner* than The Good Ship Lollipop.

The vessel's very name may prove deeply ironic, for there will be one security man to every 15 residents, homes will be ringed with electronic surveillance equipment, the ship's police will have access to firearms, the captain will have absolute power, and there will be a jail in which to dump miscreants.

A squad of intelligence officers will monitor threats to security, both from inside the ship and externally from pirates and terrorists. The ship will be equipped with 'state-of-the-art defensive weapons' to repel attacks and the system of government sounds remarkably similar to that of some of the world's least savoury regimes.

Construction is to start later this summer in Honduras. More than 15,000 labourers will work for 24 hours a day to get the ship built by 2003. Already more than a fifth of the 20,000 residential units, which cost from £80,000 to £5 million, have been sold, with sales averaging £4.7 m a week. Many have been sold to clients in Britain and Europe. The US businessmen and engineers behind the project are so confident they are already planning three more Freedom Ships.

'It is a new lifestyle for this new millennium,' said Roger Gooch, marketing director of the Freedom Ship.

The promotional literature for the project paints a magnificent picture of a luxurious tax haven that progresses steadily across the world's oceans, served by a fleet of light aircraft and speed boats. There will be shops, parks, concert halls, schools, homes and even a university on board. A huge duty-free shopping mall will generate significant revenue, it is claimed. The ship is so big – six times larger than any other vessel ever built – that a 100 ft wave will hardly affect it, the builders say.

The captain will be in a position to enforce the laws of whichever country's flag under which Gooch and his colleagues decide to sail her. Traditionally, states such as Panama have provided so-called flags of convenience, though Gooch said the ship's management were considering two European Union nations as possibilities.

The ship's private security force of 2,000, led by a former FBI agent, will have access to weapons, both to maintain order within the vessel and to resist external threats. They can expect to be kept busy, according to sociologists, maritime security experts, criminologists and intelligence experts consulted by *The Observer* last week. 'The ship will have all the problems of any small city, including crime, outbreaks of disorder, juvenile delinquency, neighbourhood disputes, everything,' said Mike Bluestone, a London-based security consultant. 'And the ship will be a prime target for terrorists. It would be perfectly possible to hold the entire vessel to ransom by seizing a few well-chosen hostages.'

Residents will be cosmopolitan, and that may not help social cohesion, says Ivan Horrocks, a security specialist at the Scarman Centre at the University of Leicester. 'When you create an artificial environment involving people with very different ethical, cultural, political and legal customs and values, the potential for tension is very great. It could well be more of a dystopia than a Utopia,' he said.

But others are more sanguine about the Freedom Ship's prospects. One of the major attractions of the vessel, according to Gooch, is its freedom from taxes. Professor Ken Roberts, a sociologist at Liverpool University, believes that if people merely use the ship as a mobile tax haven, then it could function socially. 'People who have an international occupational life might find it attractive, though I do not see people with that kind of money spending all their lives on a ship,' he said.

Others note that residents may be preoccupied with less drastic problems than the threat of piracy. Many of the first units to be sold have gone to Germans, raising the spectre of towels already on deckchairs by the time the rest of Europe's aspirant global voyagers make it to the pool.

The **active** and **passive voices** in verbs affect the meaning of a text.

object

active: The security guard checked the gates.

passive: The gates were checked by the security guard.

subject

The passive voice is not often used in speech. You will find it used in informative writing rather than in imaginative writing and is used when the writer wants an impersonal style.

Reading for meaning

1 a) What potential problems with life on the ship does the article identify?

   b) What benefits are identified?

2 a) The opening paragraph establishes a sceptical tone. How does the author do this? *Hint: Look at vocabulary, content and allusions.*

   b) The article opens with the passive voice. What effect does this achieve here?

3 The author includes quotes from other sources, both positive and negative, with regard to the ship. Identify these quotes and say which are presented most convincingly.

4 Why does the author open and close with humour? What stereotype does the writer employ to end his article in an amusing way?

5 What would you say is the purpose of this piece of journalism? Is there more than one purpose?

6 The text contains many of the features of non-fiction writing. Some of the conventions of non-fiction writing are listed in the table on page 86. Complete the table with examples from the text .

Stylistic convention	Example from text
facts and statistics	
passive voice	
quotes from interested parties	
analogy (comparing the subject to things with which the reader will already be familiar, to help put it in context)	

Sentences and paragraphs

1 Identify the paragraphs in the article that are organised with an opening topic sentence.

2 a) Comment on the effect of the use of sentences in paragraph 2.

   b) Why is paragraph 5 a single sentence?

Speaking and listening

In groups of four imagine you are involved in a marketing meeting which is discussing publicity and promotion for accommodation on board the Freedom Ship. Your slogan is 'A New Lifestyle for a New Millennium'. You are planning a brochure to tell prospective purchasers about the ship and to persuade them that life would be incomplete without an apartment on board.

- First you should consider exactly what sort of information you have to include: price, details of accommodation, facilities, security and so on.

- Then you need to consider what the strong selling points are. You need to appeal to your audience (people with lots of money who want to avoid paying taxes and want to live in an exclusive environment).

- Having considered the contents of the brochure you need to consider how best to present the information (what subsections you will have and what the design will be like).

Writing to persuade, argue and advise

Now you have had your marketing meeting, produce the brochure advertising the Freedom Ship for potential buyers.

Think about persuasive language, rhetorical features, content and design.

Writing to inform, explain and describe

Imagine you are the Education Correspondent for *The Observer*. Jason Burke, who wrote the original article about the Freedom Ship, has passed on some information to you about the educational facilities that are going to be available on board the ship for the children of those purchasing apartments.

These are Burke's notes:

> * *No qualified teachers willing to work on board, problems recruiting*
> * *Children from different countries, no shared language – will feel very isolated*
> * *Ship's facilities mainly cater for adults*
> * *Spoke with social worker, Sarah Thomas, said: 'Terrible environment for children ...'*
> * *Consultant child psychologist, Jane Brewer, said: 'Living on the ship could cause long-term social problems and feeling of isolation.'*
> * *Captain's own children will be on board; he feels it will give them a wealth of experience.*

Write an article reporting and commenting on the educational opportunities and problems for children on board the Freedom Ship.

Do some research of your own to add to the article, but use Burke's information too.

Burke's original article can also act as a model. Think of the table you completed in *Reading for meaning*. It should contain any stylistic conventions you might need. Think of the tone in which Burke wrote – impersonal, but obviously somewhat dubious about the ship.

Doctor Faustus

Doctor Faustus was written by Christopher Marlowe, a contemporary of Shakespeare; they were actually born in the same year.

The play is about a scholar called Doctor Faustus, who is frustrated by his studies. Instead he turns to magic and the occult to find knowledge, fame and power. He successfully conjures up the devil's servant Mephistopheles who, on behalf of Lucifer, persuades Faustus to sign away his soul to the devil. In return, Mephistopheles will satisfy any of Faustus's wishes for the next twenty-four years.

A good angel does try to persuade Faustus against such action, but Faustus is too eager to have his every need catered for.

The play ends with Faustus, having enjoyed the gifts of the devil, desperately pleading for God's mercy. However, it is too late, and as the clock strikes midnight Faustus is taken by devils to spend eternity in Hell.

Before you read

Our dreams of personal happiness might entail winning the lottery. If you were to sell your soul to the devil, like Faustus, what would you seek in return?

1 ....
....

2 ....
....
....
....
....

3 ....
....
....
....
....

Doctor Faustus

Act 2 Scene 1

Enter FAUSTUS in his study.

FAUSTUS. Now, Faustus, must thou needs be damned,
And canst thou not be saved.
What boots it then to think of God or heaven?
Away with such vain fancies and despair!
Despair in God and trust in Beelzebub.   5
Now go not backward. No, Faustus, be resolute.
Why waverest thou? O, something soundeth in mine ears:
'Abjure this magic, turn to God again!'
Ay, and Faustus will turn to God again.
To God? He loves thee not.   10
The god thou servest is thine own appetite,
Wherein is fixed the love of Beelzebub.
To him I'll build an altar and a church,
And offer lukewarm blood of new-born babes.

Enter GOOD ANGEL and EVIL ANGEL.

GOOD ANGEL. Sweet Faustus, leave that execrable art.   15

FAUSTUS. Contrition, prayer, repentance – what of them?

GOOD ANGEL. O, they are means to bring thee unto heaven.

EVIL ANGEL. Rather illusions, fruits of lunacy,
That makes men foolish that do trust them most.

GOOD ANGEL. Sweet Faustus, think of heaven and heavenly things. 20

EVIL ANGEL. No, Faustus; think of honour and wealth.

Exeunt ANGELS.

FAUSTUS. Of wealth?
Why, the seigniory of Emden shall be mine.
When Mephistopheles shall stand by me,
What god can hurt thee, Faustus? Thou art safe;   25
Cast no more doubts. Come, Mephistopheles,
And bring glad tidings from great Lucifer.
Is't not midnight? Come, Mephistopheles!
Veni, veni, Mephistophile!

Enter MEPHISTOPHELES.

Now tell, what says Lucifer thy lord?   30

MEPHISTOPHELES. That I shall wait on Faustus whilst he lives,
So he will buy my service with his soul.

FAUSTUS. Already Faustus hath hazarded that for thee.

MEPHISTOPHELES. But, Faustus, thou must bequeath it solemnly
    And write a deed of gift with thine own blood,   35
    For that security craves great Lucifer.
    If thou deny it, I will back to hell.
FAUSTUS. Stay, Mephistopheles, and tell me, what good will my
    soul do thy lord?
MEPHISTOPHELES. Enlarge his kingdom.   40
FAUSTUS. Is that the reason he tempts us thus?
MEPHISTOPHELES. *Solamen miseris socios habuisse doloris.*
FAUSTUS. Have you any pain, that tortures others?
MEPHISTOPHELES. As great as have the human souls of men.
    But tell me, Faustus, shall I have thy soul?   45
    And I will be thy slave, and wait on thee,
    And give thee more than thou hast wit to ask.
FAUSTUS. Ay, Mephistopheles, I give it thee.
MEPHISTOPHELES. Then stab thine arm courageously,
    And bind thy soul that at some certain day   50
    Great Lucifer may claim it as his own,
    And then be thou as great as Lucifer.
FAUSTUS.*[cutting his arm].* Lo, Mephistopheles, for love of thee
    I cut mine arm, and with my proper blood
    Assure my soul to be great Lucifer's,   55
    Chief lord and regent of perpetual night.
    View here the blood that trickles from mine arm,
    And let it be propitious for my wish.
MEPHISTOPHELES. But Faustus, thou must write it in
    manner of a deed of gift.   60
FAUSTUS. Ay, so I will. [*He writes*] But Mephistopheles,
    My blood congeals, and I can write no more.
MEPHISTOPHELES. I'll fetch thee fire to dissolve it straight.

                                  Exit.

FAUSTUS. What might the staying of my blood portend?
    Is it unwilling I should write this bill?   65
    Why streams it not, that I may write afresh?
    'Faustus gives to thee his soul' – ah, there it stayed!
    Why shouldst thou not? Is not thy soul thine own?
    Then write again: 'Faustus gives to thee his soul.'
Enter MEPHISTOPHELES with a chafer of coals.

MEPHISTOPHELES. Here's fire. Come Faustus, set it on.   70

FAUSTUS. So; now the blood begins to clear again,

    Now will I make an end immediately. [*He writes*]

MEPHISTOPHELES [*aside*] O, what will not I do to obtain his soul?

FAUSTUS. *Consummatum est*. This bill is ended,

    And Faustus hath bequeathed his soul to Lucifer.   75

    But what is this inscription on mine arm?

    'Homo, fugi!' Whither should I fly?

    If unto God, he'll throw thee down to hell. –

    My senses are deceived; here's nothing writ. –

    I see it plain. Here in this place is writ   80

    'Homo, fugi!' Yet shall not Faustus fly.

MEPHISTOPHELES.[*aside*]. I'll fetch him somewhat to delight his mind.

                                               Exit.

Enter MEPHISTOPHELES *with devils, giving crowns and rich apparel to* faustus, *and dance and then depart.*

FAUSTUS. Speak, Mephistopheles. What means this show?

MEPHISTOPHELES. Nothing, Faustus, but to delight thy mind withal

    And to show thee what magic can perform.   85

FAUSTUS. But may I raise up spirits when I please?

MEPHISTOPHELES. Ay, Faustus, and do greater things than these.

FAUSTUS. Then there's enough for a thousand souls.

    Here, Mephistopheles, receive this scroll,

    A deed of gift of body and of soul –   90

    But yet conditionally that thou perform

    All articles prescribed between us both.

MEPHISTOPHELES. Faustus, I swear by hell and Lucifer

      To effect all promises between us made

FAUSTUS. Then hear me read them.   95

    'On these conditions following:

    First, that Faustus may be a spirit in form and substance.

    Secondly, that Mephistopheles shall be his servant,
    and at his command.

    Thirdly, that Mephistopheles shall do for him   100
    and bring him whatsoever.

    Fourthly, that he shall be in his chamber or house invisible.
    Lastly, that he shall appear to the said John Faustus at all
    times in what form or shape soever he please.

I, John Faustus of Wittenberg, Doctor, by these presents, do 105
give both body and soul to Lucifer, Prince of the East, and
his minister Mephistopheles; and furthermore grant unto
them that four-and-twenty years being expired, the articles
above written inviolate, full power to fetch or carry the said
John Faustus, body and soul, flesh, blood, or goods, into 110
their habitation wheresoever.

By me, John Faustus.'

Reading for meaning

1 Write appropriate captions for each of the pictures on page 89 to convey what is happening in each scene.

W 7

2 Look at lines 6 and 7. 'To be resolute' means 'to be certain/decided' so what do you think it means when Faustus says he is wavering? What state of mind is he in at the beginning of this scene?

3 Summarise the most obvious differences between the good angel's argument and the evil angel's argument. *Hint: Think about how long the rewards that each angel offers will last and how long it will take to gain their respective rewards.*

4 What do you think Faustus's vision of his future is when he signs away his soul?

5 Why does Marlowe use words like 'service' (line 32), 'bequeath' (line 34) and 'deed of gift' (line 35) which all make the transaction seem very ordinary, everyday and businesslike?

6 Why do you think it is significant that Faustus signs the agreement in blood? *Hint: What does blood represent for us?*

7 At first Faustus's blood only trickles from his arm and then it congeals. What effect does Marlowe achieve here? *Hint: Imagine you were watching the play, what would you be thinking at this point? How does this create tension?*

8 Do you get any impression of Mephistopheles's character? *Hint: Look at what he says and the way he says it; look at how he treats Faustus; look at the asides he makes to the audience.*

Spelling and vocabulary

**W
4a)
b)**

You can often use the context of a word to help you decipher its meaning. This is a useful skill when you are dealing with pre-twentieth-century texts.

Can you decipher the meaning of the following words from their context?

- Beelzebub (line 5)
- abjure (line 8)
- execrable (line 15)
- contrition (line 16)
- bequeath (line 34)

Use a dictionary to check your ideas.

Language change

The English language has changed in many ways since Marlowe was writing.

1 a) Look at Faustus's first piece of dialogue (lines 1–14) and write down all the words that you would no longer find used in quite the same way now.

   b) Now find modern equivalents for them.

2 Write a modern version of Faustus's first piece of dialogue.

Drama

You are going to recreate the scene between Faustus and the good angel, where the angel is trying to persuade Faustus *not* to sign his soul away.

- In groups of three decide who will be the good angel, who will be Faustus and who will be an observer.

- The two characters have to think about what they could say, that would be suitable for the role they have been given.

- It is the observer's role to make notes on how the angel attempts to persuade Faustus not to sign his soul away. The observer might note down: 'angel appeals to Faustus's sense of right and wrong' or 'angel points out all the things which could go wrong'.

Once the observer has watched the two characters perform they should have a long list of persuasive techniques.

Wr 14

Writing to persuade, argue and advise

Now write the good angel's dialogue for yourself. Consider all the persuasive techniques that were noted down in *Drama* and include them. No doubt there will be others you want to add. Also try to consider the most logical order to put them in, saving your best piece of persuasion until the end.

Writing to imagine, explore and entertain

Many people have tried to update Marlowe's play:

- an episode of 'The Simpsons' in which Bart sells his soul to the devil

- the film *Bedazzled* where Liz Hurley, as the devil, tempts a young man to sell his soul.

Write an updated version of the Doctor Faustus story. Keep the basic storyline (someone selling their soul to the devil for personal gain).

You would need the same number of characters, fulfilling the same roles, but you can put them in any setting and they can be whoever you want.

Review

With a partner, explore what you have learned in this chapter.

1 Choose:
   - your best piece of work
   - your least successful piece of work.

2 Read or allow your partner to read each piece of work. Explain to your partner the reasons for your choice. Identify features which you:
   - used successfully
   - need to develop.

Focus on Reading

1 What strategies have you adopted when reading through a text for meaning? Which strategy was particularly successful?

2 How have you developed your own reading skills?

3 You have read various texts and used information to create a new piece of writing for a different purpose. What advice would you give to a fellow student who was just about to embark upon a similar task?

4 What have you learned about the use of rhetorical devices in this chapter? Where would you be able to use rhetorical devices in your own writing?

5 How difficult did you find the comparison of the different text types? What would you do differently now?

6 In the comparison you made between the styles of two different poets, what three things did you find interesting?

Base on your responses, set three targets for improving your next piece of work. You might set targets such as:

a) Read quickly through the text once, then read more carefully – for meaning – the second time

b) use notes for representing information

c) Review the use of rhetorical devices and use appropriately at least once in my own writing.

The Reading test

Preparing for Assessment Focus 4

> **Assessment Focus 4: comment on the structure and organisation of texts, including grammatical and presentational features at text level.**
>
> This assessment focus asks you to look at the way a text is organised and to explain the effect of this organisation. You could be asked to comment on how the paragraphs, punctuation, headings or choice of particular words support the development of ideas in the text. It is important to consider whether or not the organisation is typical of that text type. The questions will often ask 'how' and 'why'.

Example

The following sample questions are based on 'Freedom Ship'. Reread the text on pages 83 – 84.

a) Here are four sub-headings that could be used in the article. Number each sub-heading to show the order in which it should be placed in the text. (1 mark)

Law and order	3
Top security	1
Facilities	2
Social tension	4

Examiner's comments

This part of the question is asking how the passage is structured. The order indicated is correct because 'Top security' relates to paragraph six; 'Facilities' are described in paragraph six; 'Law and order' comes in paragraph seven, and 'Social tension' is the focus in paragraphs eight and nine.

Example

b) Explain two effects of organising the information in this way. (2 marks)

- The article starts by outlining the ship's main security features before explaining the other features. The security issue that is the focus of the article is therefore emphasised, but it isn't the only information given.

- Having given information about the precautions taken and some idea of the way of life on the ship through listing the facilities available, the likely problems are considered and the view of experts are given. This means that the reader can consider whether they also think these problems will arise. It wouldn't have been as effective if the views had been given first before the reader knows about the ship.

Examiner's comments

This part of the question is asking why the passage is structured in this way. Two different points are made about the organisation of the article and therefore both marks are awarded: the effect of listing the security features at the start is recognised (it gives emphasis to them); it is noted that the facts about the ship's features (security and other) precede the problems and opinions. An effect is given (the reader can also have an opinion). The final comment confirms understanding of this point. Note how the student has focused on the beginning and the end of the article.

Other points that could have been made instead include: the way the listing of the features is a logical development from the point made in the opening paragraph; the move from concrete facts to opinions; the inclusion of other material not linked to security in the middle of the article for contrast, to lighten the serious tone and to help emphasise the next points about security.

Practice

1 The article makes serious points about security but how does the structure of the text ensure it doesn't become too negative? Give two reasons. (2 marks)

2 Explain how the first three paragraphs are structured.
   a) What is the link between the first paragraph and the second?
   b) What is the link between the second and third paragraphs?

3 a) Look at this sentence in paragraph nine: '*When you create an artificial environment involving people with very different ethical, cultural, political and legal customs and values, the potential for tension is very great. It could well be more of a dystopia than a Utopia.*' What effect do the words used in it have?

   b) Look at this sentence from the beginning of paragraph nine: '*Residents will be cosmopolitan, and that may not help social cohesion, says Ivan Horrocks, a security specialist at the Scarman Centre at the University of Leicester.*' Why are no inverted commas used?

The Writing test

Writing to persuade, argue and advise

Example

You are invited to take part in a television programme ('Out of this World') about a community living on a space station. The facilities will be fantastic. It is a chance to do something different and you will be able to learn first hand about space. The programme needs someone who has the right personality, can explain why they are interested and who has relevant practical skills or experience.

Write a letter to the television company persuading them that you should be chosen for this once-in-a-lifetime opportunity. (30 marks)

Examiner's comments

*The main task is in **bold** print and is introduced by some information that will help you to respond. In this example, you are told the **audience** for your writing (the television company), the **purpose** of the writing (to persuade) and the **type** of writing (letter). You are also given some ideas about **content** (personality, interest, skills/experience).*

Planning

Before you start writing your response, you should spend a few minutes noting down some key points and deciding how you will organise them.

Content

For your persuasive letter you should write:

- an **opening paragraph** that explains the reason for writing, attracts the reader's attention and is persuasive
- a **concluding paragraph** that restates your main point and ends on a positive
- paragraphs that explain your reasons for applying, personal qualities and experience. This information needs to be written in a way that sustains the reader's interest and persuades. Argue your point of view.

Organisation and style

The letter requires **persuasive writing**. You will need to use:

- first person (because you are writing about yourself), active voice
- short sentences for effect after longer sentences
- formal vocabulary
- connectives related to logic ('this shows', 'because', 'therefore', 'in fact')
- value-judgement words to influence the reader ('obviously', 'vital')
- adjectives/adverbs for emotive/rhetorical effect.

Here is part of a letter written by a student in response to this task. Look at the features of persuasive writing that have been used.

Dear 'Out of this World',

I am writing to ask to be considered for the space station programme you are making. A keen space enthusiast, this is the opportunity I have been looking for and feel sure that I have the qualities you require.

My fascination with space began as a child when I first read about the moon landing and watched other space missions on television. Since then, I have longed to explore space and would relish the opportunity to live on a space station. I would also look forward to living in a different community, making new friends and being independent of my parents. I'm sure you'll agree that these are excellent reasons for applying.

Examiner's comments

*The **purpose** of the letter is immediately clear ('I am writing to ask …'). The request is made in a **formal manner** ('to be considered' and 'the qualities you require'). The content remains generalised, but the serious interest is established ('keen', 'enthusiast', 'opportunity I have been looking for'). It resists using the clichèd 'opportunity of a lifetime'. The second paragraph focuses on the different reasons for applying. It is made clear that this is a long-term interest rather than a spur of the moment whim. The enthusiasm is expressed through the choice of words like 'fascination', 'longed', 'relish' and 'look forward to'. One sentence groups the reasons into a list of 3, making it memorable and sound balanced. The paragraph then ends with a contrasting short statement that encourages the reader to feel the same way as the writer ('I'm sure you'll agree …').*

What might this student write about next? How might the letter end?

Practice

Now write your own response to this task. As you write, remember to:

- use your plan
- choose vocabulary and sentence structures carefully
- develop each point logically, adding appropriate detail
- compose in paragraphs and link the paragraphs
- keep in mind the reader of the letter.

When you have finished, remember to check your work:

- Read it through to check it is logically organised and appropriately detailed. Read each sentence carefully, looking for technical errors.

The billions of people that live on Earth divide up into smaller cultural groups. A culture shares all the knowledge, expectations and beliefs of a group or people. This chapter looks at the way some of these cultures manage themselves, the way they live and work together, and the similarities and differences between them.

3.1 Duty and virtue

The two extracts that follow look at the way two different groups of people, one Chinese and one African, regard their women.

Before you read

In small groups, discuss a situation in which you have had to sacrifice something you really liked in order to help others.

- What did you have to sacrifice?

- How did it feel when you were making the decision?

- How much did giving up that precious thing affect you?

- What effect did your decision have on others?

- Would you make that same decision again?

The Rain Came

'The Rain Came', a story by Grace Ogot, is about a father, the chief of a Kenyan tribe, who has to make a very difficult decision about his daughter's future, a decision upon which the lives of his people depend ...

The Rain Came

The chief was still far from the gate when his daughter Oganda saw him. She ran to meet him. Breathlessly she asked her father, 'What is the news, great Chief? Everyone in the village is anxiously waiting to hear when it will rain.' Labong'o held out his hands for his daughter but he did not say a word. Puzzled by her father's cold attitude Oganda ran back to the village to warn others that the chief was back.

The atmosphere in the village was tense and confused. Everyone moved aimlessly and fussed in the yard without actually doing any work. A young woman whispered to her co-wife, 'If they have not solved this rain business today, the chief will crack.' They had watched him getting thinner and thinner as the people kept on pestering him. 'Our cattle lie dying in the fields,' they reported. 'Soon it will be our children and then ourselves. Tell us what to do to save our lives, oh great Chief.' So the chief had daily prayed with the Almighty through the ancestors to deliver them from their distress.

Instead of calling the family together and giving them the news immediately, Labong'o went to his own hut, a sign that he was not to be disturbed. Having replaced the shutter, he sat in the dimly lit hut to contemplate.

It was no longer a question of being the chief of a hunger-stricken people that weighed Labong'o's heart. It was the life of his only daughter that was at stake. At the time when Oganda came to meet him, he saw the glittering chain shining around her waist. The prophecy was complete. 'It is Oganda, Oganda, my only daughter, who must die so young.' Labong'o burst into tears before finishing the sentence. The chief must not weep. Society had declared him the bravest of men. But Labong'o did not care any more. He assumed the position of a simple father and wept bitterly. He loved his people, the Luo, but what were the Luo for him without Oganda? Her life had brought a new life in Labong'o's world and he ruled better than he could remember. How would the spirit of the village survive his beautiful daughter? 'There are so many homes and so many parents who have daughters. Why choose this one? She is all I have.' Labong'o spoke as if the ancestors were there in the hut and he could see them face to face. Perhaps they were there, warning him to remember his promise on the day he was enthroned when he said aloud, before the elders, 'I will lay down life, if necessary, and the life of my household, to save this tribe from the hands of the enemy.' 'Deny! Deny!' he could hear the voice of his forefathers mocking him.

When Labong'o was consecrated chief he was only a young man. Unlike his father, he ruled for many years with only one wife. But people rebuked him because his only wife did not bear him a daughter. He married a second, a third, and a fourth wife. But they all gave birth to male children. When Labong'o married a fifth wife she bore him a daughter. They called her Oganda, meaning 'beans', because her skin was very fair. Out of Labong'o's 20 children, Oganda was the only girl. Though she was the chief's favourite, her mother's co-wives swallowed their jealous feelings and showered her with love. After all, they said, Oganda was a female child whose days in the royal family were numbered. She would soon marry at a tender age and leave the enviable position to someone else.

Never in his life had he been faced with such an impossible decision. Refusing to yield to the rainmaker's request would mean sacrificing the whole tribe, putting the interests of the individual above those of the society. More than that. It would mean disobeying the ancestors, and most probably wiping the Luo tribe from the surface of the earth. On the other hand, to let Oganda die as a ransom for the people would permanently cripple Labong'o spiritually. He knew he would never be the same chief again.

The words of Ndithi, the medicine man, still echoed in his ears. 'Podho, the ancestor of the Luo, appeared to me in a dream last night,

105

and he asked me to speak to the chief and the people,' Ndithi had said to the gathering of tribesmen. 'A young woman who has not known a man must die so that the country may have rain. While Podho was still talking to me, I saw a young woman standing at the lakeside, her hands raised, above her head. Her skin was as fair as the skin of young deer in the wilderness. Her tall slender figure stood like a lonely reed at the river bank. Her sleepy eyes wore a sad look like that of a bereaved mother. She wore a gold ring on her left ear, and a glittering brass chain around her waist. As I still marvelled at the beauty of this young woman, Podho told me, "Out of all the women in this land, we have chosen this one. Let her offer herself a sacrifice to the lake monster! And on that day, the rain will come down in torrents. Let everyone stay at home on that day, lest he be carried away by the floods."'

Outside there was strange stillness, except for the thirsty birds that sang lazily on the dying trees. The blinding midday heat had forced the people to retire to their huts. Not far away from the chief's hut, two guards were snoring away quietly. Labong'o removed his crown and the large eagle-head that hung loosely on his shoulders. He left the hut, and instead of asking Nyabog'o the messenger to beat the drum, he went straight and beat it himself. In no time the whole household had assembled under the siala tree where he usually addressed them. He told Oganda to wait a while in her grandmother's hut. When Labong'o stood to address his household, his voice was hoarse and the tears choked him. He started to speak, but words refused to leave his lips. His wives and sons knew there was great danger. Perhaps their enemies had declared war on them. Labong'o's eyes were red, and they could see he had been weeping. At last he told them. 'One whom we love and treasure must be taken away from us. Oganda is to die.' Labong'o's voice was so faint, that he could not hear it himself. But he continued, 'The ancestors have chosen her to be offered as a sacrifice to the lake monster in order that we may have rain.'

They were completely stunned. As a confused murmur broke out, Oganda's mother fainted and was carried off to her own hut. But the other people rejoiced. They danced around singing and chanting, 'Oganda is the lucky one to die for the people. If it is to save the people, let Oganda go.'

Reading for meaning

1 a) What do we learn about the relationship between Oganda and her father in the opening paragraph of the story?

b) How do we know that Labong'o, the father, is worried?

Use quotation from the text to support your answers.

2 a) What do you learn about this culture's attitude to marriage?

b) Why do you think they follow this custom?

3 a) As chief, what responsibilities does Labong'o have to his people?

b) What do his people think of him?

c) How do they treat him?

4 a) Who is Ndithi and what is his role within this society?

b) Why has Labong'o been to see him?

5 a) Labong'o is the chief of the tribe. What does he wear which symbolises his leadership?

b) Why do you think he removes these outward symbols before he summons the household?

6 a) What does the manner in which Labong'o addresses his household tell us about the way he feels about his daughter?

b) In what ways is the response of the rest of the household unusual?

7 Why do you think Labong'o, the chief, intends to follow what Ndithi says?

Now read on ...

In her grandmother's hut Oganda wondered what the whole family were discussing about her that she could not hear. Her grandmother's hut was well away from the chief's court and, much as she strained her ears, she could not hear what was said. 'It must be marriage,' she concluded. It was an accepted custom for the family to discuss their daughter's future marriage behind her back. A faint smile played on Oganda's lips as she thought of the several young men who swallowed saliva at the mere mention of her name.

There was Kech, the son of a neighbouring clan elder. Kech was very handsome. He had sweet, meek eyes and a roaring laughter. He would make a wonderful father, Oganda thought. But they would not be a good match. Kech was a bit too short to be her husband. It would humiliate her to have to look down at Kech each time she spoke to him. Then she thought of Dimo, the tall young man who had already distinguished himself as a brave warrior and an outstanding wrestler. Dimo adored Oganda, but Oganda thought he would make a cruel husband, always quarrelling and ready to fight. No, she did not like him. Oganda fingered the glittering chain on her waist as she thought of Osinda. A long time ago when she was quite young Osinda had given her that chain, and instead of wearing it around her neck several times, she wore it round her waist where it could stay permanently. She heard her heart pounding so loudly as she thought of him. She whispered, 'Let it be you they are discussing, Osinda, the lovely one. Come now and take me away ...'

The lean figure in the doorway startled Oganda who was rapt in thought about the man she loved. 'You have frightened me, Grandma,' said Oganda laughing. 'Tell me, is it my marriage you were discussing? You can take it from me that I won't marry any of them.' A smile played on her lips again. She was coaxing the old lady to tell her quickly, to tell her they were pleased with Osinda.

In the open space outside the excited relatives were dancing and singing. They were coming to the hut now, each carrying a gift to put at Oganda's feet. As their singing got nearer Oganda was able to hear what they were saying: 'If it is to save the people, if it is to give us rain, let Oganda go. Let Oganda die for her people, and for her ancestors.' Was she mad to think that they were singing about her? How could she die? She found the lean figure of her grandmother barring the door. She could not get out. The look on her grandmother's face warned her that there was danger around the corner. 'Mother, it is not marriage then?' Oganda asked urgently. She suddenly felt panicky like a mouse cornered by a hungry cat. Forgetting that there was only one door in the hut Oganda fought desperately to find another exit. She must fight for her life. But there was none.

She closed her eyes, leapt like a wild tiger through the door, knocking her grandmother flat to the ground. There outside in mourning garments Labong'o stood motionless, his hands folded at the back. He held his daughter's hand and led her away from the excited crowd to the little red-painted hut where her mother was resting. Here he broke the news officially to his daughter.

For a long time the three souls who loved one another dearly sat in darkness. It was no good speaking. And even if they tried, the words could not have come out. In the past, they had been like three cooking stones, sharing their burdens. Taking Oganda away from them would leave two useless stones which would not hold a cooking-pot.

News that the beautiful daughter of the chief was to be sacrificed to give the people rain spread across the country like the wind. At sunset the chief's village was full of relatives and friends who had come to congratulate Oganda. Many more were on their way coming, carrying their gifts. They would dance till morning to keep her company. And in the morning they would prepare her a big farewell feast. All these relatives thought it a great honour to be selected by the spirits to die, in order that the society may live. 'Oganda's name will always remain a living name among us,' they boasted.

But was it maternal love that prevented Minya from rejoicing with the other women? Was it the memory of the agony and pain of child-birth that made her feel so sorrowful? Or was it the deep warmth and understanding that passes between a suckling babe and her mother that made Oganda part of her life, her flesh? Of course it was an honour, a great honour, for her daughter to be chosen to die for the country. But what could she gain once her only daughter was blown away by the wind? There were so many other women in the land, why choose her daughter, her only child! Had human life any meaning at all – other women had houses full of children while she, Minya, had to lose her only child!

Reading for meaning

1 a) Why does Labong'o call his household to a meeting?

   b) What does Oganda think the reason is?

   c) What are her feelings as she waits for her father in the hut?

2 When Oganda realises that there is something wrong, how does she behave? To what is she compared? Use quotation from the text in your answer.

3 Oganda spends some time with her mother and father, alone in the 'little red-painted hut'. To what are they compared and why do you think the author uses this comparison?

4 Why do you think the relatives were 'excited' and brought gifts to Oganda?

5 How does Minya's attitude to the sacrifice differ from that of the relatives?

Now read on ...

In the cloudless sky the moon shone brightly, and the numerous stars glittered with a bewitching beauty. The dancers of all age-groups assembled to dance before Oganda, who sat close to her mother, sobbing quietly. All these years she had been with her people she thought she understood them. But now she discovered that she was a stranger among them. If they loved her as they had always professed why were they not making any attempt to save her? Did her people really understand what it felt like to die young? Unable to restrain her emotions any longer, she sobbed loudly as her age-group got up to dance. They were young and beautiful and very soon they would marry and have their own children. They would have husbands to love and little huts for themselves. They would have reached maturity. Oganda touched the chain around her waist as she thought of Osinda. She wished Osinda was there too, among her friends. 'Perhaps he is ill,' she thought gravely. The chain comforted Oganda – she would die with it around her waist and wear it in the underground world.

In the morning a big feast was prepared for Oganda. The women prepared many different tasty dishes so that she could pick and choose. 'People don't eat after death,' they said. Delicious though the food looked, Oganda touched none of it. Let the happy people eat. She contented herself with sips of water from a little calabash.

The time for her departure was drawing near, and each minute was precious. It was a day's journey to the lake. She was to walk all night, passing through the great forest. But nothing could touch her, not even the denizens[1] of the forest. She was already anointed with sacred oil. From the time Oganda received the sad news she had expected Osinda to appear at any moment. But he was not there. A relative told her that Osinda was away on a private visit. Oganda realised that she would never see her beloved again.

In the afternoon the whole village stood at the gate to say good-bye and to see her for the last time. Her mother wept on her neck for a long time. The great chief in a mourning skin came to the gate bare-footed, and mingled with the people – a simple father in grief. He took off his wrist bracelet and put it on his daughter's wrist saying, 'You will always live among us. The spirit of our forefathers is with you.'

Tongue-tied and unbelieving Oganda stood there before the people. She had nothing to say. She looked at her home once more. She could hear her heart beating so painfully within her. All her childhood plans were coming to an end. She felt like a flower nipped in the bud never to enjoy the morning dew again. She looked at her weeping mother, and whispered, 'Whenever you want to see me, always look at the sunset. I will be there.'

Oganda turned southwards to start her trek to the lake. Her parents, relatives, friends and admirers stood at the gate and watched her go.

Her beautiful slender figure grew smaller and smaller till she mingled with the thin dry trees in the forest. As Oganda walked the lonely path that wound its way in the wilderness, she sang a song, and her own voice kept her company.

The ancestors have said Oganda must die
The daughter of the chief must be sacrificed,
When the lake monster feeds on my flesh,
The people will have rain.
Yes, the rain will come down in torrents.
And the floods will wash away the sandy beaches

1 Inhabitants

When the daughter of the chief dies in the lake.
My age-group has consented
So have my friends and relatives.
Let Oganda die to give us rain.
My age-group are young and ripe,
Ripe for womanhood and motherhood
But Oganda must die young,
Oganda must sleep with the ancestors.
Yes, rain will come down in torrents.

The red rays of the setting sun embraced Oganda, and she looked like a burning candle in the wilderness.

The people who came to hear her sad song were touched by her beauty. But they all said the same thing: 'If it is to save the people, if it is to give us rain, then be not afraid. Your name will forever live among us.'

At midnight Oganda was tired and weary. She could walk no more. She sat under a big tree, and having sipped water from her calabash, she rested her head on the tree trunk and slept.

When Oganda woke up in the morning the sun was high in the sky. After walking for many hours, she reached the tong', a strip of land that separated the inhabited part of the country from the sacred place (kar lamo). No layman could enter this place and come out alive – only those who had direct contact with the spirits and the Almighty were allowed to enter this holy of holies. But Oganda had to pass through this sacred land on her way to the lake, which she had to reach at sunset.

A large crowd gathered to see her for the last time. Her voice was now hoarse and painful, but there was no need to worry any more. Soon she would not have to sing. The crowd looked at Oganda sympathetically, mumbling words she could not hear. But none of them pleaded for life. As Oganda opened the gate, a child, a young child, broke loose from the crowd, and ran towards her. The child took a small earring from her sweaty hands and gave it to Oganda saying, 'When you reach the world of the dead, give this earring to my sister. She died last week. She forgot this ring.' Oganda, taken aback by the strange request, took the little ring, and handed her precious water and food to the child. She did not need them now. Oganda did not know whether to laugh or cry. She had heard mourners sending their love to their sweethearts, long dead, but this idea of sending gifts was new to her.

Reading for meaning

1 a) What confuses Oganda as she sits and watches the dancers?

 b) What does she regret most?

 c) Why do you think Oganda doesn't eat anything at the feast?

2 a) When Oganda embarks upon her journey, what protects her from the spirits of the forest?

 b) Why does her father give Oganda his wrist bracelet?

3 As Oganda leaves the village, the reader feels tremendous sympathy and admiration for her. How does the author create that response in the reader?

4 What is unusual about the attitude of the villagers to Oganda's fate? Use reference to text in your answer.

5 Why does Oganda sing as she walks?

6 What do you think will happen to Oganda when she reaches her final destination?

Now read on ...

Oganda held her breath as she crossed the barrier to enter the sacred land. She looked appealingly at the crowd, but there was no response. Their minds were too preoccupied with their own survival. Rain was the precious medicine they were looking for, and the sooner Oganda could get to her destination the better.

 A strange feeling possessed Oganda as she picked her way in the sacred land. There were strange noises that often startled her, and her first reaction was to take to her heels. But she remembered that she had to fulfil the wish of her people. She was exhausted, but the path was still winding. Then suddenly the path ended on sandy land. The water had retreated miles away from the shore leaving a wide stretch of sand. Beyond this was the vast expanse of water.

Oganda felt afraid. She wanted to picture the size and shape of the monster, but fear would not let her. The society did not talk about it, nor did the crying children who were silenced by the mention of its name. The sun was still up, but it was no longer hot. For a long time Oganda walked ankle-deep in the sand. She was exhausted and longed desperately for her calabash of water. As she moved on, she had a strange feeling that something was following her. Was it the monster? Her hair stood erect, and a cold paralysing feeling ran along her spine. She looked behind, sideways and in front, but there was nothing, except a cloud of dust.

Oganda pulled up and hurried but the feeling did not leave her, and her whole body became saturated with perspiration.

The sun was going down fast and the lake shore seemed to move along with it.

Oganda started to run. She must be at the lake before sunset. As she ran she heard a noise coming from behind. She looked back sharply, and something resembling a moving bush was frantically running after her. It was about to catch up with her.

Oganda ran with all her strength. She was now determined to throw herself into the water even before sunset. She did not look back, but the creature was upon her. She made an effort to cry out, as in a nightmare, but she could not hear her own voice. The creature caught up with Oganda. In the utter confusion, as Oganda came face to face with the unidentified creature, a strong hand grabbed her. But she fell flat on the sand and fainted.

When the lake breeze brought her back to consciousness, a man was bending over her. '.......!' Oganda opened her mouth to speak, but she had lost her voice. She swallowed a mouthful of water poured into her mouth by the stranger.

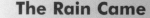

'Osinda! Osinda! Please let me die. Let me run, the sun is going down. Let me die, let them have rain.' Osinda fondled the glittering chain around Oganda's waist and wiped the tears from her face.

'We must escape quickly to the unknown land,' Osinda said urgently. 'We must run away from the wrath of the ancestors and the retaliation of the monster.'

'But the curse is upon me, Osinda, I am no good to you any more. And moreover the eyes of the ancestors will follow us everywhere and bad luck will befall us. Nor can we escape from the monster.'

Oganda broke loose, afraid to escape, but Osinda grabbed her hands again.

'Listen to me, Oganda! Listen! Here are two coats!' He then covered the whole of Oganda's body, except her eyes, with a leafy attire made from the twigs of the Bwombwe. 'These will protect us from the eyes of the ancestors and the wrath of the monster. Now let us run out of here.' He held Oganda's hand and they ran from the sacred land, avoiding the path that Oganda had followed.

The bush was thick, and the long grass entangled their feet as they ran. Halfway through the sacred land they stopped and looked back. The sun was almost touching the surface of the water. They were frightened. They continued to run, now faster, to avoid the sinking sun.

'Have faith, Oganda – that thing will not reach us.'

When they reached the barrier and looked behind them trembling, only a tip of the sun could be seen above the water's surface.

'It is gone! It is gone!' Oganda wept, hiding her face in her hands.

'Weep not, daughter of the chief. Let us run, let us escape.'

There was a bright lightning. They looked up, frightened. Above them black furious clouds started to gather. They began to run. Then the thunder roared, and the rain came down in torrents.

115

Reading for meaning

1 Using at least five adjectives, describe how Oganda was feeling as she entered the sacred land.

2 In what ways does the author build up a sense of tension as Oganda walks towards the lake?

3 Why is Oganda reluctant to leave with Osinda?

4 What is the significance of the last paragraph?

Vocabulary

1 What is unusual about the language of the Kenyan tribe? How does it compare to standard English? You should look at both the combinations of letters and the use of punctuation marks.

2 a) Investigate the meanings of the following words: bungalow, khaki, monsoon, kebab, jungle.

b) From which ancient languages do the majority of English words originate?

Speaking and listening

S&L 9

Imagine that Oganda and Osinda arrive back at the village after the rains have fallen. They want to be taken back into the village, get married and have a family. The tribal council meets to make a decision about whether or not to allow this.

In groups, role-play the meeting of the tribal council. One of the council members should be the chief, Labong'o. Take into consideration the cultural information you have gained from the story.

Research

R 7

The story of 'The Rain Came' involves a pretty girl being sacrificed to a horrible monster. What story from British culture is very similar to this? *Hint: Think of the patron saint of England.*

1 Find a copy of this story, using either the Internet or the library.

2 In pairs, read through the version of this story that you have found and compare it to 'The Rain Came'. What similarities and differences are there?

Writing to inform, explain and describe

Using your knowledge of the story of 'The Rain Came', design a web page for the BBC's 'Natural World' website.

- This page should include information about the Luo tribe, their customs, beliefs and way of life.

- In your design, you should include headings, graphics, different fonts, links to other relevant sites plus any other appropriate detail.

Writing to persuade, argue and advise

Labong'o was chosen as chief because of his bravery and courage. Faced with the sacrifice of his daughter, he is torn between his role as a father and his duty as a chief. Write a monologue in which he presents to Oganda's mother the arguments he needs to consider before making his final decision.

'Nu Jie' or Lessons for Women

This extract comes from an instructional manual on feminine behaviour and virtue written by a woman called Ban Zhao in the first century AD. She was married at the age of 14, becoming the lowest-ranking member of her husband's family. At that time, China followed the ideas and teachings of the philosopher Confucius (551–479 BC). The Confucian doctrine or religion by which Chinese society lived regarded women as of lesser status and therefore little was written in Confucian texts to give women specific and practical guidelines for everyday life. Ban Zhao sought to fill that gap with a clear and coherent set of rules for women, especially young women.

Before you read

Think about the story 'The Rain Came'.

1 What were the duties expected of Oganda and the other women in her tribe?

2 How does this compare with what is expected of women in British culture:

   a) at the beginning of the twentieth century

   b) at the beginning of the twenty-first century?

'Nu Jie' or Lessons for Women
HUMILITY

On the third day after the birth of a girl the ancients observed three customs: first to place the baby below the bed; second to give her a potsherd[1] with which to play; and third to announce her birth to her ancestors by an offering. Now to lay the baby below the bed plainly indicated that she is lowly and weak, and should regard it as her **primary** duty to humble herself before others. To give her potsherds with which to play **indubitably** signified that she should practise labour and consider it her primary duty to be industrious. To announce her birth before her ancestors clearly meant that she ought to esteem as her primary duty the continuation of the observance of worship in the home.

These three ancient customs **epitomise** woman's ordinary way of life and the teachings of the traditional ceremonial **rites** and regulations. Let a woman modestly yield to others; let her respect others; let her put others first, herself last. Should she do something good, let her not mention it; should she do something bad, let her not deny it. Let her bear disgrace; let her even endure when others speak or do evil to her. Always let her seem to tremble and to fear. When a woman follows such **maxims** as these then she may be said to humble herself before others.

Let a woman retire late to bed, but rise early to duties; let her not dread tasks by day or by night. Let her not refuse to perform domestic duties whether easy or difficult. That which must be done, let her finish completely, tidily and systematically. When a woman follows such rules as these, then she may be said to be industrious.

Let a woman be correct in manner and upright in character in order to serve her husband. Let her live in purity and quietness of spirit, and attend to her own affairs. Let her love not gossip and silly laughter. Let her cleanse and purify and arrange in order the wine and the food for the offerings to the ancestors. When a woman observes such principles as these, then she may be said to continue ancestral worship.

No woman who observes these three **fundamentals** of life has ever had a bad reputation or has fallen into disgrace. If a woman fail to observe them, how can her name be honoured; how can she but bring disgrace upon herself?

1 A piece of broken pottery

Reading for meaning: 'Humility'

1 a) What are the three customs that were followed after the birth of a girl?

   b) Choose one word to describe the qualities associated with these three customs.

2 What is a woman supposed to do in order to demonstrate these qualities?

3 What does Ban Zhao consider to be the outcome of observing these instructions?

Now read on ...

Reading for meaning: 'Husband and Wife'

1 Look up the terms 'yin' and 'yang' in a dictionary *and* an encyclopaedia. What are the characteristics of these elements? You should use the information provided in this text as well as the reference books to write a full description.

2 a) What is the attitude to marriage in Chinese society at this time?

   b) What are the roles of men and women in a marriage?

   c) How does this compare with the attitude of the Luo tribe to marriage in 'The Rain Came'?

3 Read the last paragraph again. What argument is Ban Zhao trying to express to the 'gentlemen of the present age'? What does she believe should happen?

HUSBAND AND WIFE

The Way of husband and wife is intimately connected with Yin and Yang and relates the individual to gods and ancestors. Truly it is the great **principle** of Heaven and Earth, and the great basis of human relationships. Therefore the 'Rites' honour union of man and woman; and in the 'Book of Poetry' the 'First Ode' manifests the principle of marriage. For these reasons the relationships cannot but be an important one.

If a husband be unworthy, then he possesses nothing by which to control his wife. If a wife be unworthy, then she possesses nothing with which to serve her husband. If a husband does not control his wife, then the rules of conduct **manifesting** his authority are abandoned and broken. If a wife does not serve her husband, then the proper relationship between men and women and the natural order of things are neglected and destroyed. As a matter of fact the purpose of these two [the controlling of women by men, and the serving of men by women] is the same.

Now examine the gentlemen of the present age. They only know that wives must be controlled, and that the husband's rules of conduct manifesting his authority must be established. They therefore teach their boys to read books and study histories. But they do not in the least understand that husbands and masters must also be served, and that the proper relationship and the rites should be maintained. Yet only to teach men and not to teach women – is that not ignoring the essential relation between them? According to the 'Rites', it is the rule to begin to teach children to read at the age of eight years, and by the age of fifteen years they ought then to be ready for cultural training. Only why should it not be that girls' education as well as boys' be according to this principle?

WOMANLY QUALIFICATIONS

A woman ought to have four qualifications: (1) womanly virtue; (2) womanly words; (3) womanly bearing; and (4) womanly work. Now what is called womanly virtue need not be brilliant ability, exceptionally different from others. Womanly words need be neither clever in debate nor keen in conversation. Womanly appearance requires neither a pretty nor a perfect face and form. Womanly work need not be work done more skilfully than that of others.

To guard carefully her **chastity**; to control **circumspectly** her behaviour; in every motion to exhibit modesty; and to model each act on the best usage, this is womanly virtue.

To choose her words with care; to avoid vulgar language; to speak at appropriate times; and not to weary others with much conversation, may be called the characteristics of womanly words.

To wash and scrub filth away; to keep clothes and ornaments fresh and clean; to wash the head and bathe the body regularly, and to keep the person free from disgraceful filth, may be called the characteristics of womanly bearing.

With whole-hearted devotion to sew and to weave; to love not gossip and silly laughter; in cleanliness and order to prepare the wine and food for serving guests, may be called the characteristics of womanly work.

These four qualifications characterise the greatest virtue of a woman. No woman can afford to be without them. In fact they are very easy to possess if a woman only treasure them in her heart. The ancients had a saying: 'Is love afar off? If I desire love, then love is at hand!' So can it be said of these qualifications.

Reading for meaning: 'Womanly Qualifications'

1 Describe the four qualities of women that Ban Zhao considers important.

2 What does Ban Zhao mean when she uses the example of the saying from 'the ancients': 'Is love afar off? If I desire love, then love is at hand!'?

Vocabulary and spelling

1 Find **synonyms** for the following words:

primary, indubitably, epitomise, rites, maxims, fundamentals, principle, manifesting, chastity, circumspectly.

2 a) What is the dictionary definition of the word 'circumspectly'?

b) From which language does this word originate?

3 a) The roots of the word 'circumspectly' are 'circum' and 'specere'. What does each mean?

b) Give two other words (plus their meanings) which use the prefix 'circum-'.

c) Using a dictionary to help you, find two words which come from the root 'specere' and give their meaning.

Paragraphs and sentences

1 Look again at the section headed 'Humility' (page 119).

a) How has Ban Zhao organised her thoughts?

b) What other types of writing are organised in a similar fashion?

2 In the section 'Humility', a large number of sentences begin with the words 'Let a woman …' or 'Let her …'. What is unusual about this opening? What effect does the repetition of this phrase have?

3 Consider the remaining two sections: 'Husband and Wife' (page 121) and 'Womanly Qualifications' (page 122). How does Ban Zhao organise her ideas and thoughts?

a) What types of sentence openings does she use?

b) Does she use similar techniques to the first section?

Comparing texts: understanding the author's craft

'Lessons for Women' is a non-fiction text, whereas 'The Rain Came' is a fictional legend from the oral tradition of Grace Ogot's people.

1 What do you learn about the standpoint and views of both writers?

2 In what ways are they similar or different?

3 Write three paragraphs to compare the standpoint and views of the two texts.

Speaking and listening

1 In small groups, discuss the following statements:

a) A woman's place is in the home.

b) The man's role in a marriage is to earn the money.

c) Marriage is an equal partnership.

d) The woman's vow to 'love, honour and obey' should be included in a marriage ceremony.

Summarise your group's views to the rest of the class.

2 Again in small groups, discuss the three aspects of womanly behaviour advised upon in 'Lessons for Women'.

• Identify the characteristics of womanly behaviour.

• List those characteristics which your group feel are relevant to marriage and today's society.

Writing to persuade, argue and advise

Produce a leaflet for the woman of today, in which you outline the ways in which a woman should conduct herself within a relationship. You could, if you wish, produce a **parody** of the original advice given by Ban Zhao.

> **Parody** is an imitation of a piece of writing in which the writer sets out to ridicule or make fun of the original. The parody in literature is equivalent to the cartoon or caricature in art.

Writing to analyse, review and comment

What have you learned about the different cultures identified in 'The Rain Came' and 'Lessons for Women'?

- How do they compare to your own society?

- What lessons, if any, should we be taking from these cultures?

Write an extended essay in which you reflect on your own society, making comparisons with other cultures and presenting ideas for the future.

3.2 When different cultures meet

> Groups of people are rarely isolated from one another. Many different cultures make up the peoples of Britain. Some people and their families have lived in Britain as long as they can remember, and even further back. Some people were born and brought up in Britain, but have parents or grandparents who come from a different culture. Some people moved to Britain from elsewhere as children or adults. This section looks at the way different cultures come together.

S&L 2

Speaking and listening

- Do you live in the country where you were born?
- Can you speak more than one language?
- What individual qualities do you have?
- What sort of food do you eat?
- How important is your family to you?
- What different groups of people do you belong to?
- What would you say is your 'way of life'?

Share your thoughts with a partner. Discuss the meaning of the term 'culture'.

- What does it mean?
- What is the British 'culture'?

126

Inglan Is A Bitch

This poem is written by a man born in Jamaica, a former British colony. Linton Kwesi Johnson was born in Chapelton in 1952. His mother washed clothes and his father was a baker and sugar estate worker. His parents separated when Johnson was seven and his mother emigrated to London, leaving her son with his grandparents. Johnson eventually joined his mother in Brixton, London when he was eleven.

Speaking and listening

The poem is written in non-standard English.

1 Read through the poem silently.

2 Working in pairs, develop a reading of the poem that will help others to understand the meaning.

- Use the rhyme and rhythm of the lines.

- Think about the music of reggae and rap artists and the way they deliver their songs.

Reading for meaning

1 a) When the narrator first came to London, what job did he do?

  b) What is unusual about the effect this particular job had on his life?

2 a) What other jobs has the narrator done?

  b) What does his willingness to undertake these types of jobs tell us about his personality?

3 What does the narrator single out as the biggest problems of living and working in England?

4 The narrator says 'dem seh dat black man is very lazy' (line 35). Who does 'dem' refer to?

5 How would you describe the narrator's feelings about England?

6 Who do you think this poem is addressing? Give reasons for your answer.

7 What does this poem make you think about? Have your opinions about anything changed?

Inglan Is A Bitch

w'en mi jus' come to Landan toun
mi use to work pan di andahgroun
but workin' pan di andahgroun
y'u don't get fi know your way around

Inglan is a bitch   5
dere's no escapin it
Inglan is a bitch
dere's no runnin' whey fram it

mi get a lickle jab in a bih 'otell
an' awftah a while, mi woz doin' quite well   10
dem staat mi aaf as a dish-washah
but w'en mi tek a stack, mi noh tun clack-watchah

Inglan is a bitch
dere's no escapin it
Inglan is a bitch   15
no baddah try fi hide fram it

w'en dem gi' you di lickle wage packit
fus dem rab it wid dem big tax rackit
y'u haffi struggle fi mek en's meet
an' w'en y'u goh a y'u bed y'u jus' can't sleep   20

Inglan is a bitch
dere's no escapin it
Inglan is a bitch
a noh lie mi a tell, a true

mi use to work dig ditch w'en it cowl noh bitch   25
mi did strang like a mule, but bwoy, mi did fool
den awftah a while mi jus' stap dhu ovahtime
den awftah a while mi jus' phu dung mi tool

Inglan is a bitch
dere's no escapin it   30
Inglan is a bitch
y'u haffi know how fi survive in it

well mi dhu day wok an' mi dhu nite wok
mi dhu clean wok an' mi dhu dutty wok
dem seh dat black man is very lazy   35
but if y'u si how mi wok y'u woulda sey mi crazy

Inglan is a bitch
dere's no escapin it
Inglan is a bitch
y'u bettah face up to it   40

dem a have a lickle facktri up inna Brackly
inna disya facktri all dem dhu is pack crackry
fi di laas fifteen years dem get mi laybah
now awftah fifteen years mi fall out a fayvah

Inglan is a bitch   45
dere's no escapin it
Inglan is a bitch
dere's no runnin' whey fram it

mi know dem have work, work in abundant
yet still, dem mek mi redundant   50
now, at fifty-five mi gettin' quite ol'
yet still, dem sen' mi fi goh draw dole

Inglan is a bitch
dere's no escapin it
Inglan is a bitch   55
is whey wi a goh dhu 'bout it?

Linton Kwesi Johnson

R
16

Standard English

Linton Kwesi Johnson comes from Jamaica and writes as he would speak in a Jamaican **patois**, using **phonetic spelling**.

> **Patois** is a dialect, or form of language, which is spoken in a particular area or part of a country.
>
> **Phonetic spelling** means that a word is written down as it sounds. For example: 'aw rite mite' is the phonetic equivalent of a commonly used greeting 'all right mate', as spoken in the south of England.

1 In what ways is Johnson's Jamaican patois different from standard English?

2 Compile a list of statements about the way that language is used in this poem. For example: The letters 'th' are replaced by the letter 'd'.

   You should consider the phonetic spelling as well as the punctuation and the grammar.

3 a) Choose two consecutive verses and 'translate' them into standard English.

   b) Compare your standard English verses with the original verses. What can you say about the effect the use of patois has?

4 What influences, if any, has Jamaican patois had on the English language? Have any words or expressions been adopted into the English language, or become commonly used as slang?

Johnson's poetic technique

This poem is an example of **dub poetry** or **reggae poetry**. These terms have come to be applied to Johnson's own poetry.

* What form does the poet use in this poem?

* How is the poem organised?

* In what way does the poet use rhyme and rhythm in the poem?

* What do you notice about every second verse? What effect does this have on the way the poem sounds?

> **Dub poetry** and **reggae poetry** are both terms coined by Linton Kwesi Johnson to describe Jamaican DJs 'toasting' (speaking, rapping, rhyming) over the B-sides of reggae songs.

Writing to imagine, explore and entertain

The poem describes one man's experience of England.

1 Choose one of the moments or experiences described in the main verses of the poem. For example: just arriving in England and working on the London Underground.

Think about the moment you have chosen, using ideas from the rest of the poem upon which to base your thoughts.

- What were the narrator's feelings and reactions?
- What were his job conditions like?
- How did others respond to him?
- Where did he live?
- How did he get to work?
- What hours did he work?
- What did he earn?
- How does life in England differ from that in his original home?

2 Discuss your ideas with a partner, then write a lively and imaginative account of this experience.

You might start by describing the weather. For example:

'Cold. Raw cold that seeped through the thickest layers to numb the heart.'

This type of opening is more dramatic and interesting than writing:

'It was very cold and I couldn't wear enough clothes.'

If you use a variety of sentence lengths and vivid vocabulary your writing will be more interesting.

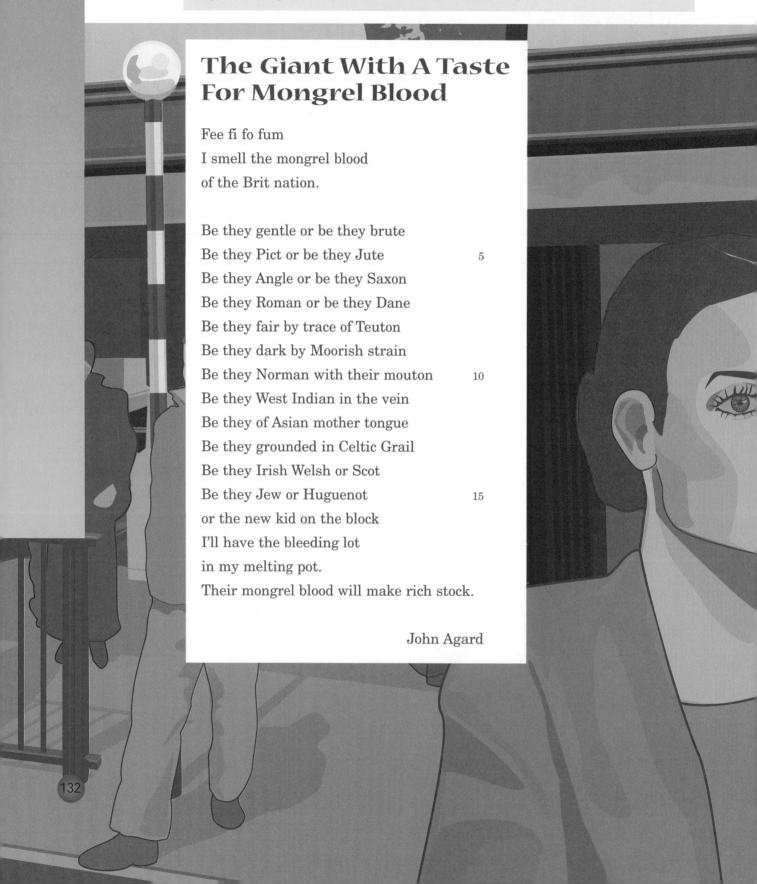

John Agard is another Caribbean poet, born in Georgetown, the capital of Guyana. He moved to Britain in 1977.

The Giant With A Taste For Mongrel Blood

Fee fi fo fum
I smell the mongrel blood
of the Brit nation.

Be they gentle or be they brute
Be they Pict or be they Jute   5
Be they Angle or be they Saxon
Be they Roman or be they Dane
Be they fair by trace of Teuton
Be they dark by Moorish strain
Be they Norman with their mouton   10
Be they West Indian in the vein
Be they of Asian mother tongue
Be they grounded in Celtic Grail
Be they Irish Welsh or Scot
Be they Jew or Huguenot   15
or the new kid on the block
I'll have the bleeding lot
in my melting pot.
Their mongrel blood will make rich stock.

John Agard

Reading for meaning

1 The term 'mongrel' is used in the title.

   a) To what does this term usually refer and what does it mean?

   b) What is the connotation of the word?

   c) What is the connotation of the abbreviation 'Brit'?

2 a) Who is speaking in the poem?

   b) To what other literary text does John Agard link this poem?

   c) Why do you think he opens the poem in the way he does?

3 What does the poet say are the ingredients for the British nation? List these ingredients and identify their origins.

4 Why do you think the poet uses the phrase 'bleeding lot' (line 17)? He also refers to blood a number of times in the poem. Why does he do this?

5 What is the message the poet wants to get across to the reader? What does this poem leave you thinking about? Have your opinions about anything changed?

6 In what ways are the poems in this section by John Agard and Linton Kwesi Johnson similar?

Agard's poetic technique

1 John Agard performs his poetry and therefore he uses sound to create effect. In what ways is sound used in this poem? What is the effect?

2 a) What do you notice about the punctuation of Agard's poem?

   b) What punctuation marks might you expect to be included?

   c) Rewrite the poem, inserting the appropriate punctuation marks you have discussed.

   d) Read the poem out loud. What effect does this have on the poem?

   e) Why does the poet use punctuation in this way?

3 Consider the two poems in this section again. What similarities and differences are there in:

   a) the content

   b) the form

   c) the rhyme and rhythm

   d) the way in which language and punctuation are used?

133

Writing to persuade, argue and advise

Using the ideas expressed by John Agard in this poem, write an article for a student newspaper in which you argue that the society of the future will be stronger and richer because of the many cultures that contribute to it.

Speaking and listening

In pairs, prepare an interview with either John Agard or Linton Kwesi Johnson. You are going to interview the poet on a radio programme for teenagers.

1 You should decide:

   • which of you will be the poet and which the presenter

   • what type of radio show it will be – music, current affairs, literary?

   • what style of programme it will be – serious, light-hearted?

   • what the name of the programme will be

   • how you are going to introduce the interview.

2 Develop the questions for your interview. Your aim is to ask questions to inform your listeners about the poet himself and the poem he has written.

3 Role-play the interview.

White Teeth

This extract is taken from a novel by Zadie Smith about 'three cultures and three families over three generations'. This particular section reflects on how society has changed and how it affects the characters in the novel.

The following characters are mentioned in the extract:

- Alsana and Samad Iqbal – A Bengali couple who have twin sons, Millat and Magid.

- Clara Jones – Clara is Jamaican. She and her white English husband Archie have a daughter, Irie.

- Hortense Bowden – Clara's mother.

- The Chalfen family – A very white English family. The father, Marcus, is a scientist; the mother, Joyce, is a writer and looks after the family of four boys.

White Teeth

This has been the century of strangers, brown, yellow and white. This has been the century of the great immigrant experiment. It is only this late in the day that you can walk into a playground and find Isaac Leung by the fish pond, Danny Rahman in the football cage, Quang O'Rourke bouncing a basketball, and Irie Jones humming a tune. Children with first and last names on a direct collision course. Names that secrete within them mass exodus, cramped boats and planes, cold arrivals, medical checks. It is only this late in the day, and possibly only in Willesden, that you can find best friends Sita and Sharon, constantly mistaken for each other because Sita is white (her mother liked the name) and Sharon is Pakistani (her mother thought it best – less trouble). Yet, despite all the mixing up, despite the fact that we have finally slipped into each other's lives with reasonable comfort (like a man returning to his lover's bed after a midnight walk), despite all this, it is still hard to admit that there is no one more English than the Indian, no one more Indian than the English. There are still young men who are angry about that; who will roll out at closing time into the poorly lit streets with a kitchen knife wrapped in a tight fist.

But it makes an immigrant laugh to hear the fears of the nationalist, scared of infection, penetration, miscegenation, when this is small fry, peanuts, compared to what the immigrant fears – dissolution, disappearance. Even the unflappable Alsana Iqbal would regularly wake up in a puddle of her own sweat after a night visited by visions of Millat (genetically BB; where B stands for Bengali-ness) marrying someone called Sarah (aa where 'a' stands for Aryan), resulting in a child called Michael (Ba), who in turn marries somebody called Lucy (aa), leaving Alsana with a legacy of unrecognizable great-grandchildren (Aaaaaaa!), their Bengali-ness thoroughly diluted, genotype hidden by phenotype. It is both the most irrational and natural feeling in the world. In Jamaica, it is even in the grammar: there is no choice of personal pronoun, no splits between me or you or they, there is only the pure, homogenous I.

When Hortense Bowden, half white herself, got to hearing about Clara's marriage, she came round to the house, stood on the doorstep, said, 'Understand: I and I don't speak from this moment forth,' turned on her heel and was true to her word. Hortense hadn't put all that effort into marrying black, into dragging her genes back from the brink, just so her daughter could bring yet more high-coloured children into the world.

Likewise, in the Iqbal house the lines of battle were clearly drawn. When Millat brought an Emily or a Lucy back home, Alsana quietly wept in the kitchen, Samad went into the garden to attack the coriander. The next morning was a waiting game, a furious biting of tongues until the Emily or Lucy left the house and the war of words could begin. But with Irie and Clara the issue was mostly unspoken, for Clara knew she was not in a position to preach. Still, she made no attempt to disguise her disappointment or the aching sadness. From Irie's bedroom shrine of green-eyed Hollywood idols to the gaggle of white friends who regularly trooped in and out of her bedroom, Clara saw an ocean of pink skins surrounding her daughter and she feared the tide that would take her away.

It was partly for this reason that Irie didn't mention the
Chalfens to her parents. It wasn't that she intended to mate
with the Chalfens … but the instinct was the same. She had
a nebulous fifteen-year-old's passion for them, overwhelming,
yet with no real direction or object. She just wanted to, well,
kind of, merge with them. She wanted their Englishness.
Their Chalfishness. The purity of it. It didn't occur to her that
the Chalfens were, after a fashion, immigrants too (third
generation, by way of Germany and Poland, née
Chalfenovsky), or that they might be as needy of her as she
was of them. To Irie, the Chalfens were more English than
the English. When Irie stepped over the threshold of the
Chalfen house, she felt an illicit thrill, like a Jew munching a
sausage or a Hindu grabbing a Big Mac. She was crossing
borders, sneaking into England; it felt like some terribly
mutinous act, wearing somebody else's uniform or somebody
else's skin.

She just said she had netball on Tuesday evenings and
left it at that.

Vocabulary and spelling

Look up the words 'genotype' and 'phenotype' in the dictionary. They are very similar in meaning. In pairs, discuss the difference in meaning between them.

Reading for meaning

1 a) What is the significance of the names used in the first five lines of the text?

   b) Why did the parents of Sita and Sharon choose these particular names for their children?

2 a) What does the author mean by writing 'there is no one more English than the Indian, no one more Indian than the English'?

   b) Why does this make young men angry?

   c) How do they express their anger?

3 a) A nationalist fears 'infection, penetration, miscegenation'. The immigrant fears 'dissolution, disappearance'. Explain in your own words, what each of them fears.

   b) Why does the 'immigrant laugh to hear the fears of the nationalist'?

4 a) What fears do Alsana and Samad Iqbal have about their son Millat's future?

   b) Clara Jones has a similar problem with her daughter, Irie. How does Clara feel? How is her situation different to the Iqbal's?

5 Read the section starting 'Even the unflappable Alsana Iqbal …', on page 136, up to '… their Bengali-ness thoroughly diluted, genotype hidden by phenotype.'

   a) What is it that gives Alsana Iqbal sleepless nights? Explain her fears in your own words.

   b) In what ways is this 'both the most irrational and natural feeling in the world'?

6   Why doesn't Irie talk about her friendship with the Chalfens? Where is the **irony** in her admiration of them?

7   'She was crossing borders, sneaking into England; it felt like some terribly mutinous act, wearing somebody else's uniform or somebody else's skin.'

   a) What do these lines tell us about how Irie feels?

   b) Why does she make the excuse about netball?

> **Irony** refers to a circumstance where the reality is different from the actual representation. For example: Antony insists that 'Brutus is an honourable man' in the Shakespeare play 'Julius Caesar'.

Standard English

1   Read the section starting 'In Jamaica …', on page 136, up to '… turned on her heel and was true to her word.'

   a) What is unusual about the grammar of the Jamaican dialect?

   b) Translate what Hortense says to Clara into standard English.

2   Write a short piece of dialogue between Hortense and another person, in which you use this same Jamaican grammatical form. Hortense is discussing the marriage of her daughter to an Englishman. *Hint: Write the dialogue in standard English first.*

Writing to analyse, review and comment

Wr 16

Consider the similarities and differences between this prose extract from 'White Teeth' and the poem, 'The Giant With A Taste For Mongrel Blood' (page 132). Write an extended essay in which you compare:

• form

• content

• language

• message.

Going for an English

In *White Teeth*, Zadie Smith writes '*that there is no one more English than the Indian, no one more Indian than the English*'. In the following sketch from the comedy series 'Goodness Gracious Me', the writer satirises a stereotypical British activity, going for a curry after a night in the pub. Two young Indian men and two young Indian girls go for 'an English' at an 'English' restaurant in India.

Satire is a form of writing in which the writer criticises something, for example an attitude or institution, by using criticism blended with humour and wit.

Going for an English

Friday night, a Berni Inn[1] in downtown Bombay, just after the pubs have shut.

Loud belch

young man 1:	Oh, I'm totally off my face. How come every Friday night we end up in the Berni Inn?
young man 2:	Because that's what you do isn't it. You go out to get tanked up on lassis[2] and you go for an English.
Ira:	And anyway I love English food, yaah.
man 2:	Oh get off. You just fancy the waiter innit.
Ira:	No. [*She laughs*]
Nina:	Shhh. He's coming, he's coming.
man 2:	Here we go. [*With exaggerated care*] Alright mite. [*In a cockney accent*] Ha. [*Laughs*]
Ira:	Hello.
man 2:	We're ready to order now. What …
	Loud belch
Ira:	He's alright this waiter. He's a mate you know. [*Loudly with attempt at exaggerated cockney accent*] I say you're a mite [*mate*] ain't you Jamez? [*She giggles*] Jamez is my mite. [*Then in normal voice*] What? Jamez, yah that's what I said. Goddamit!
Nina:	Hasn't he got lovely pale skin yaah, it's really nice and tasty isn't it?
Ira:	Yaah.
Nina:	And you know what they say about white men don't you. [*Both women laugh and say ooohh*]
man 2:	Alright alright, what are we having?
man 1:	Right, Jamez. First up we'll have what ten, twelve.

Voices as the others interrupt, calling out different numbers.

---

1 A chain of steakhouses, started in 1955, rebranded in 1990 as Beefeater pubs
2 An Indian drink made from fresh fruit, milk, milk curds, a touch of spice, served cold with crushed ice

Ira:	No, make it twelve.
Nina:	Yah yah.
man 1:	Alright twelve bread rolls.
man 2:	Also bring us a dish of that erm, what's it …, what's the …
Ira:	Dunno.
man 1:	It's butter.
man 2:	Ah, butter as well. Okay, main course, what's everyone want?
man 1:	What is the blandest thing on the menu?

Others exclaim.

man 1:	Scam-pie is it? And that's totally tasteless yeah? Right, I'll have that and gimme plenty of that ketchup.

Others chorus 'Ohhhh'.

man 2:	Yeah, well I'll have the same as him right, but I'll have a prawn cocktail with it.

Others chorus exclamations.

Ira:	You will regret that in the morning!
man 2:	What are you having, Nina?
Nina:	Er, could I just er have the chicken curry.
Ira:	Oh God, Nina.
man 1:	Nina, come on it's an English restaurant. You've got to have something English, no spices shisses.
Nina:	Oh Nitin. You know I don't like it too bland.
man 2:	Well, have something that is just a bit bland.
Ira:	Yaah.
man 2:	Hey Jamez what have you got that is not totally tasteless yeah yeah? There you go, steak and kidney p. Have that, Nina.
Nina:	But you know what it does to me, it blocks me right up, I won't go to the toilet for a week.
man 2:	Exactly yaah, now that's the point of having an English isn't it?

Nina:	Hey what are you having, Ira?
Ira:	Oh God, I can't decide right between the steak and kidney p., or the cod de mornay.
Nina:	I'll tell you what, you have the p., I'll have the cod and we can mix and match.
Ira:	Okay yaah, yaah. I think that's the way you're supposed to eat this sort of food anyway isn't it?
man 1:	So that's two scam-pies, one cod de mornay.
Nina:	Yaah, yaah.
man 1:	And a steak and kidney p.
Ira:	Yaah.
man 2:	Chips?
man 1:	Four chips.

Others' voices interspersed suggesting numbers.

man 1:	So, that will be twenty-four plates of chips.
man 2:	What do you mean too much food?
man 1:	Who asked you? Just bring us the blinking food or I'll do a mooney.

Reading for meaning

1 Why has the writer chosen to set this sketch in a Berni Inn? What are the characteristics of this type of restaurant?

2 Why do the Indian characters 'get tanked up on lassis'? Why do they not drink alcohol?

3 a) In pairs, discuss and identify the activities and attitudes being satirised. Use a table like the one below to record your ideas.

Comment in sketch (satire)	Actual activity/attitude being satirised
You go out to get tanked up on lassis and you go for an English	You drink lager to get drunk and you go for an Indian

b) What attitude is being illustrated by this sketch?

4 Why do you think the sketch ends with the threat to 'do a mooney'?

5 a) In what ways is the audience intended to respond to this sketch?

b) Is the satire intended to be hurtful?

c) What is the purpose of the satire?

6 a) When Nina says 'And you know what they say about white men don't you.', both women laugh. Why do they both laugh?

b) This is an example of 'innuendo'. What do you think the term 'innuendo' means? Give your own example of innuendo.

Writing to imagine, explore and entertain

Rewrite this sketch, changing the details so that it portrays the English activity of going for a curry after spending the evening in the pub on a Friday. You should start your script as follows:

voiceover: *Friday night, a curry house in London, just after the pubs have shut.*

Trevor: [*Loud belch*]
Oh, I'm totally off my face. How come every Friday night we end up in the curry house?

Speaking and listening

You are going to perform both versions of 'Going for an English': the one printed in this book and one of the scripts you wrote in *Writing to imagine, explore and entertain*.

- In groups of six, read through the two versions of the script for this sketch.

- Choose one person to direct the piece.

- Develop a dramatic performance of the sketch.

- Consider tone of voice, volume, movement, gesture and facial expression.

Drama

1 Perform both versions of the sketch for the rest of the class.

2 As you watch other groups perform their versions of the sketch, note down which elements are humorous. Which of the two sketches is funnier? Why?

Sn 3

Writing to analyse, review and comment

Write a review of 'Going for an English' for the entertainment section of a newspaper.

Your review should be 150 words long and contain comment on the context, the content and the quality of the sketch.

Wr 9

Writing to inform, explain and describe

What have you learned about different cultures from the extracts you have studied in this chapter?

Write an essay which includes:

• an explanation of what a 'culture' is

• some examples of areas where different cultures might have different customs

• some examples of the attitudes that are expressed to these different customs

• some examples of what we can learn from other cultures

• a summary of the type of thing different cultures can learn from each other.

Use the extracts in this chapter to support your argument as well as your own ideas.

Review

With a partner, explore what you have learned in this chapter.

1 Choose:
   • your best piece of work
   • your least successful piece of work.

2 Read or allow your partner to read each piece of work. Explain to your partner the reasons for your choice. Identify features which you:
   • used successfully
   • need to develop.

Focus on Writing for different purposes and checking for accuracy

1 List the different purposes for which you have written. What have you learned about writing for different purposes? How does the purpose affect the way in which you write?

2 What different narrative styles have you adopted? Which style was easiest to adopt? Which style was most difficult to adopt?

3 Choose two examples of different narrative styles from your own writing. Read them through with a partner and discuss the effectiveness of your style. How could you improve your use of narrative style?

4 When you have worked within a limited time frame, what skills and techniques have you had to employ? What is the most important thing to remember when writing a timed essay?

5 What techniques have you learned to use when writing to persuade your audience? Select three examples from your own writing.

6 How have you checked your work for errors? Why is technical accuracy important in any writing?

Set three targets for improving your next piece of work. You might set targets such as:

a) Read through my work backwards to help identify errors

b) Experiment with a different narrative style

c) Plan my writing more carefully.

The Reading test

Preparing for Assessment Focus 5

Assessment Focus 5: comment on the writer's use of language, including grammatical and literary features at word and sentence level.

This assessment focus asks you to analyse the effects of writers' choices of language. This might involve the study of particular sentence structures or the effects of individual words or phrases. You will be asked either to select examples from the text that demonstrate a certain effect or explain the effect of words quoted.

The questions will often ask you to 'explain', say 'why' or comment. You could also be asked to 'find and copy', but this will usually need to be followed by an explanation. The language questions are mostly worth 1 or 2 marks.

Example

The following sample questions are based on 'Going for an English'. Reread the text on pages 142–144.

1a) **In the line: '*Also bring us a dish of that erm, what's it ...,what's the ...*', what is the purpose of the ellipses [...]? (1 mark)**

It shows the sentence is incomplete because the speaker is trying to think of the word he wants.

Examiner's comments

The explanation recognises that there are words missing, represented by the [...] and therefore gains 1 mark. The explanation also suggests understanding that the [...] represents a pause while the speaker is thinking.

b) **In the line: '*We're ready to order now. What ...*', what different purpose does the ellipsis [...] serve? (1 mark)**

In this line, the [...] shows that the speaker doesn't get to complete his sentence (because he is cut off by the loud belch).

Examiner's comments

This explanation recognises that this sentence is incomplete, not because the speaker is struggling for words, but because he has been interrupted by the sudden noise. It gains 1 mark.

Example

c) **What is the effect of using ellipses? (1 mark)**

It makes the dialogue sound real because we do have pauses in conversations and people don't finish their sentences.

Examiner's comments

This is another full explanation. 1 mark is awarded for the explanation that ellipses make the dialogue sound natural/realistic. The second part of the explanation (because ...) provides the examples to clarify the explanation.

Example

2 **Find two examples of non-standard English and explain the effect. (2 marks)**

'totally off my face': This makes the speech sound up to date because this is a popular thing to say.

'ain't': this is a short way of saying 'are not'. It makes the text sound like real speech, because we shorten words when we speak to make them quicker and easier to say.

Examiner's comments

*1 mark is awarded for each relevant quotation and explanation, up to a maximum of 2 marks. The first example chosen is an informal expression ('totally off my face'); 'get tanked up' could have been chosen instead. 1 mark is awarded because the **quotation is appropriate** and a **suitable explanation** has been given. Other explanations include: it has impact because it is informal; it is amusing because you don't expect to see phrases like this written down. The example is also used because the speaker is trying to shock the staff at the restaurant and impress his friends.*

The second example is a shortened form. There are many other examples that could have been chosen. For example: 'innit'; 'gimme'; 'dunno'. The explanation successfully makes the point that these words are easier to say than the full version, and can be said more quickly. Other responses might note that 'ain't' sounds informal but is appropriate because it is speech. 1 mark is given for this second part of the task, giving a total of 2.

Practice

These two questions are phrased differently from the sample questions above, but are asking quite similar things.

1 Why does the writer use words like 'er', 'erm', 'right' and 'yah'? (1 mark)

2 How does the writer make the dialogue sound like genuine speech? Explain two examples, remembering to quote from the text. (2 marks)

The Writing test

Writing to analyse, review and comment

Example

A book about the treatment of men and women in modern society is being published and you have been asked to contribute. You will need to analyse situations where there is equal treatment and where there is not.

Write a formal essay discussing views for and against the statement: Are men and women treated equally in today's world? (30 marks)

- **Include evidence and examples to illustrate the points**
- **Conclude with a reasoned argument for or against.**

Examiner's comments

*The main task is given in **bold** print and is introduced by some information that will help you to respond. In this example, you are told the **audience** for your writing (readers of the book), the **purpose** of the writing (analyse), the **type** of writing (discursive essay) and the **style** of the writing (formal). You are also given some ideas about **content** (views for and against).*

Content

For your discursive essay, you should write:

- an **opening paragraph** that sets out the main focus of the argument
- **paragraphs that advance each point**, either for or against, supported by examples to illustrate the argument. You should present a balanced view
- a **conclusion** that advances your own point of view.

Organisation and style

- You could write about all the points for the issue and then all the points against before explaining your own view in the conclusion. Alternatively, you could make one point for, then counter the argument in the next paragraph.

- The essay is **discursive** writing. You will need to use the features of this text type:
  - active voice is mainly used. Some use of the passive where it is not relevant to say what everyone is doing ('it could be argued that'; 'it has been claimed that')
  - the connectives linking the ideas together are about logic ('as a result', 'alternatively', 'however') and contrast/comparison ('whereas', 'however', 'similarly')
  - rhetorical questions might be asked
  - vocabulary of value judgements ('certainly', 'totally', 'entirely').

Here is part of an essay written by a student in response to this task. Look at the features of discursive writing that have been used.

There have been numerous stories of inequality between men and women in the past, but does it remain an injustice in the modern world? Many would agree that women are not treated much more fairly, but there may still be aspects of life where enough progress has not been achieved. On the other hand, it should be considered whether the attempt to redress the balance has actually led to discrimination against men.

Great improvements have been made in modern times to ensure equality between men and women in the workplace. Traditionally male occupations, like the building trade and Armed Forces are now open to women and the contribution women can make has been recognised. In Britain women are now allowed to fly planes in the RAF and we have even had a female Prime Minister. What remains true is that many women don't necessarily want the sort of work that is traditionally male and therefore they will always be under-represented in those areas.

Examiner's comments

The essay starts with an overview of the main issues from both points of view. Past changes are recognised and the central question is whether enough has yet been achieved. Rhetorical questions are asked that invite the reader to begin considering his/her own response. The connectives relate to contrast ('On the other hand ...') and, in the second paragraph, logic ('What remains true is ...'). The second paragraph introduces the first point supporting the argument. Examples are given (building trade, Armed Forces) to support the points. There is a mixture of passive voice ('has been recognised') where the people doing this do not need to be identified and direct involvement of the reader through the choice of pronouns ('we have even had').

What might this student write about next? How might the essay end?

Practice

Now write your own response to this task. As you write, remember to:
- use your plan and choose vocabulary and sentence structures carefully
- develop each point logically, adding appropriate detail
- compose in paragraphs and link the paragraphs
- keep in mind the reader of the essay.

When you have finished, remember to check your work:
- Read it through to check it is logically organised and appropriately detailed
- Read each sentence carefully, looking for technical errors.

Drama and the spoken word

4

This chapter contains extracts from texts which are about exciting, frightening and testing human experiences. The scenes, extracts and stories you will read demonstrate that the world can be a hostile, difficult and unpredictable place. You will read, write, speak, listen to and think about ideas such as:

- how relationships alter when faced with discrimination

- how people behave under interrogation

- how leaders try to inspire their people in times of war

- how a man might cope with being changed into an insect.

Most of all, you will be given the opportunity to act out and write scripts, and to invent and perform your own improvisations and speeches.

EXIT

Interpreting drama: Brecht and Beckett

The Jewish Wife

Bertolt Brecht, a German playwright, was one of the most influential dramatists of the twentieth century. *The Jewish Wife* comes from a series of scenes called *Fear and Misery of the Third Reich* which describe aspects of life in Hitler's Germany. Brecht was a political writer, who believed that plays should bring about social change by altering the opinions of the audience.

The Jewish Wife is about a Jewish woman who is agonising over whether she should leave Germany, and her non-Jewish husband, in order to protect herself, and to protect her husband's job as a doctor. The scene starts with the wife rehearsing what she is going to say to her husband, whilst packing. The play finishes with the couple's conversation.

R 2
Wr 9

Before you read

1 Using the Internet, textbooks and history books, research the laws passed by Hitler's government against Jews in the 1930s. *The Jewish Wife* is set in 1935.

a) Prepare a timeline of the laws passed in the 1930s against Jews.

b) Write a factsheet tracing the years between 1933, when Hitler came to power, and 1939, when the Second World War started. When presenting your factsheet take care over:

- font size
- text layout
- bullet points
- italics.

2 As a class, discuss the topic of discrimination.

- Brainstorm the effects of the different laws that you found out about in question 1.
- Select three key conclusions that sum up the opinions of the class.
- Use standard English to explain and justify your ideas, ensuring that you have taken everyone's comments into consideration.

As you read

1 a) How does the woman prepare herself for her meeting with her husband?

b) What is the effect of the **monologue** on the audience?

c) Why does Brecht want to prepare us for the **duologue**?

2 With a partner, read the **duologue** out loud. Try out a number of different tones of voice for the two characters.

3 Why do you think Brecht divides the scene into two sections: the monologue and duologue?

A **monologue** is a scene in drama in which a person speaks alone, whereas a **duologue** is a dramatic piece for two actors.

The Jewish Wife

Woman alone packing a case with clothes.

THE WOMAN: Yes, I'm packing. Don't pretend you haven't noticed anything the last few days. Nothing really matters, Fritz, except just one thing: if we spend our last hour together without looking at each other's eyes. That's a triumph they can't be allowed, the liars who force everyone else to lie. Ten years ago when somebody said no one would think I was Jewish, you instantly said yes, they would. And that's fine. That was straightforward. Why take things in a roundabout way now? I'm packing so they shan't take away your job as senior physician. And because they've stopped saying good morning to you at the clinic, and because you're not sleeping nowadays. I don't want you to tell me I mustn't go. And I'm hurrying because I don't want to hear you telling me I must. It's a matter of time. Principles are a matter of time. They don't last for ever, any more than a glove does. There are good ones which last a long while. But even they only have a certain life. Don't get the idea that I'm angry. Yes, I am. Why should I always be understanding? What's wrong with the shape of my nose and the colour of my hair? I'm to leave the town where I was born just so they don't have to go short of butter. What sort of people are you, yourself included? You work out the quantum theory and the Trendelenburg test, then allow a lot of semi-barbarians to tell you you're to conquer the world but you can't have the woman you want. The artificial lung, and the dive-bomber! You are monsters or you pander to monsters. Yes, I know I'm being unreasonable, but what good is reason in a world like this? There you sit watching your wife pack and saying nothing. Walls have ears, is that it? But you people say nothing. One lot listens and the other keeps silent. To hell with that. I'm supposed to keep silent too. If I loved you I'd keep silent. I truly do love you. Give me those underclothes. They're suggestive. I'll need them. I'm 36, that isn't too old, but I can't do much more experimenting. The next time I settle in a country things can't be like this. The next man I get must be allowed to keep me. And don't tell me you'll send me money; you know you won't be allowed to. And you aren't to pretend it's just a matter of four weeks either. This business is going to last rather more than four weeks. You know that, and so do I. So don't go telling me 'After all it's only for two or three weeks' as you hand me the fur coat I shan't need till next winter. And don't let's speak about disaster. Let's speak about disgrace. Oh, Fritz!

She stops. A door opens. She hurriedly sees to her appearance. The husband comes in.

THE HUSBAND: What are you doing? Tidying up?

THE WOMAN: No.

THE HUSBAND: Why are you packing?

THE WOMAN: I want to get away.

THE HUSBAND: What are you talking about?

THE WOMAN: We did mention the possibility of my going away for a bit. It's no longer very pleasant here.

THE HUSBAND: That's a lot of nonsense.

THE WOMAN: Do you want me to stay, then?

THE HUSBAND: Where are you thinking of going?

THE WOMAN: Amsterdam. Just away.

THE HUSBAND: But you've got nobody there.

THE WOMAN: No.

THE HUSBAND: Why don't you wish to stay here? There's absolutely no need for you to go so far as I'm concerned.

THE WOMAN: No.

THE HUSBAND: You know I haven't changed, you do, don't you, Judith?

THE WOMAN: Yes.

He embraces her. They stand without speaking among the suitcases.

THE HUSBAND: And there's nothing else makes you want to go?

THE WOMAN: You know that.

THE HUSBAND: It might not be such a bad idea, I suppose. You need a breather. It's stifling in this place. I'll come and collect you. As soon as I get across the frontier, even if it's only for two days, I'll start feeling better.

THE WOMAN: Yes, why don't you?

THE HUSBAND: Things can't go on like this all that much longer. Something's bound to change. The whole business will die down again like an inflammation – it's a disaster, it really is.

THE WOMAN: Definitely. Did you run into Schöck?

THE HUSBAND: Yes, just on the stairs, that's to say. I think he's begun to be sorry about the way they dropped us. He was quite embarrassed. In the long run they can't completely sit on filthy intellectuals like us. And they won't be able to run a war with a lot of spineless wrecks. People aren't all that standoffish if you face up to them squarely. What time are you off, then?

THE WOMAN: Nine-fifteen.

THE HUSBAND: And where am I to send money to?

THE WOMAN: Let's say poste restante, Amsterdam main Post-Office.

THE HUSBAND: I'll see they give me a special permit. Good God, I can't send my wife off with ten marks a month. It's all a lousy business.

THE WOMAN: If you can come and collect me it'll do you a bit of good.

THE HUSBAND: To read a paper with something in it for once.

THE WOMAN: I rang Gertrud. She'll see you're all right.

THE HUSBAND: Quite unnecessary. For two or three weeks.

THE WOMAN *who has again begun packing*:

Do you mind handing me my fur coat?

THE HUSBAND *handing it to her*:

After all it's only for two or three weeks.

Reading for meaning

1 a) Reread the text and think carefully about the dramatic relationship Brecht has created between the couple.

   b) Fill in the first two columns of a table like the one below to show how the wife says things to herself in her monologue, which neither she nor her husband are able to say directly to each other.

   c) Fill in the third column to explain why the characters can **think,** but not **speak** these things.

Comment in monologue	Evidence of same topic in duologue	Why topic is dealt with differently in duologue
This business is going to last rather more than four weeks … don't go telling me 'After all it's only for two or three weeks' as you hand me the fur coat I shan't need till next winter.'	WOMAN: Do you mind handing me my fur coat? HUSBAND handing it to her: After all it's only for two or three weeks.	Both have accepted that the wife will be leaving. Both know that they may not see each other again, but cannot say that to each other. Easier to pretend that they may only be separated for a few weeks.

2 The husband is against his wife leaving at first, but changes his mind. Explain why the husband changes his tone after the stage direction: 'He embraces her. They stand without speaking among the suitcases.'

Sentences and punctuation

Look closely at the way Brecht uses the structure of his sentences throughout the scene to create dramatic atmosphere and tension.

1 Why are there lots of short, undeveloped comments near the start of the duologue? Find five examples of one- or two-word sentences in the scene, before the stage direction 'He embraces her.'

2 In the second half of the scene the atmosphere seems to change and the tension breaks. How does Brecht alter the sentence structures to achieve this change?

Drama

If you were playing the part of the wife how would you prepare yourself for performance? Select six of her sentences from the text.

In a table like the one below:

- write in the first column the quotations from the text

- note in the second column what you will be doing on stage (movements, facial expressions, tone of voice)

- in column three analyse your performance to explain what you are trying to demonstrate about her character.

Section of text	Practical staging suggestion	Analysis
I want to get away.	She does not make eye contact with her husband. She carries on folding a cardigan that she is packing. She uses a quick, matter-of-fact, monotone voice.	She is embarrassed about being caught packing, and she tries to avoid revealing the extent of the emotion she is feeling by not stopping what she is doing, and by not looking at him.

Wr 5

Writing to imagine, explore and entertain

Predict the immediate future of the relationship of the two characters from *The Jewish Wife* by writing an exchange of four postcards, two by each character. Start with the wife (Judith) after she has arrived in Amsterdam.

- Imitate the way Brecht changes his sentence lengths, and uses questions to create dramatic atmosphere and tension.

- Experiment by using different **sentence types** in your writing.

- Explore a change in the feelings of the two characters, and answer the questions and comments made in each of the previous postcards.

The woman's first postcard may include:

- what Amsterdam is like
- where she is living
- asking how Gertrud (his sister) is looking after him
- how she is managing for money.

Statements, **questions**, **exclamations** and **commands** are all different **sentence types**. For example:

- **Statement** ('I am living in a flat in Amsterdam.')
- **Question** ('How are you coping with Gertrud?')
- **Exclamation** ('O, how I miss you!')
- **Command** ('Come to visit me soon.')

Drama: Writing a script

You are going to write your own short play preceded by a monologue, in the same style as *The Jewish Wife*. Try to create a sense of action, character, atmosphere and tension.

- Your play should be about the difficulties parents have with their teenage children.

- The situation (given below) is a parent waiting up for their child to come home after an evening out.

- The title is '***The Parent***'.

- Before you write the scene, work with a partner and **improvise** the situation together.

You are a parent. It is past midnight and you are waiting up for your teenage son or daughter who is late home again. You do not communicate well with your son or daughter but really love them and often argue with them.

Writing to advise

You are directing a performance of *The Jewish Wife*. You have written a set of preparatory notes for the actor playing the role of the husband. Write a paragraph on each of the following points, giving an example from the text in each:

- what the husband feels about his wife
- what the husband feels about his wife leaving
- how he might be costumed, or what props he might use
- how the husband might move
- what the husband's voice might be like
- how the husband's mood alters during the course of the scene.

Speaking and listening

1 Now you have read and written about *The Jewish Wife*, as a whole class discuss what you think of racial prejudice in general.

2 Brecht was a political writer who wanted to influence the beliefs of his audiences. What do you think he wants us to think of the anti-Semitism he depicts in *The Jewish Wife*. Find examples from the text to support your ideas.

What Where

The following scene is an extract from 'What Where' which is a short play by the Irish playwright Samuel Beckett. Beckett's work was considered to be experimental, and was sometimes called '*absurd*'.

In this extract, an interrogator is interrogated.

Before you read

1   In pairs, produce a series of **tableaux** which best represent the titles or captions below.

- You should take about two minutes to discuss, prepare and be ready to present each **tableau**.

- Think carefully about your body language and the **status** of the two characters in each image. For example: the character with the higher status might be on a higher level/point a finger/lean over or towards their partner; the character with the lower status might be physically lower/bow their head/assume a closed or turned-in body position.

a) '*The Telling Off*'
b) '*Caught Red-Handed*'
c) '*The Police Interview*'
d) '*Where's Your Homework?*'

2   Working with the same partner, improvise the scenes from pages 164–165 on the theme of interrogation.

- Remember to use the same elements of **non-verbal communication** that you did in the **tableaux** you produced in question 1.

- Think about your tone of voice. The character with the higher status might speak in a stronger voice/use more questions/speak more slowly/control the pace of the scene by using pauses; the character with the lower status might speak quite quickly, with a weak, defensive tone of voice/allow their partner to control the pace.

- Write an evaluation of how effectively you and your partner were able to demonstrate the differences in status in each scene.

a) 'Aunty's Chocolates'

Character A	Character B
You are the parent who has come home to find that the expensive box of chocolates you have bought for Aunty's birthday has been opened and eaten. All that remains is the empty box. You suspect Character B, who is your son or daughter, because they have arrived home early from school today.	You are the son or daughter. You arrived home from school early, found the box of chocolates and, innocently assuming that they were for the whole family, you ate them, ALL. You don't want to admit it, so you must blame anyone you can think of, and pretend that they had already been eaten when you arrived home from school. Try your older brother or sister, who might have come home from school at lunchtime, or the cat who is very clever and loves chocolate!

b) 'The Broken Window'

Character A	Character B
You are a teacher. You are on duty at lunchtime. You hear a crash and walk around the corner of a building to see Character B, a pupil, standing near a broken window, with a stone in his/her hand. You immediately assume that you have caught the guilty party.	You are a pupil. It is lunchtime. You hear a crash, and walk around the corner to find a broken window. You stoop to pick up the stone which you think must have broken it, when Character A, a teacher, comes around the corner of the building to find you. You are innocent.

c) 'The Holiday Snaps'

Character A	Character B
You are an officer in the secret police. You are interrogating Character B, a holiday-maker, whose camera has been found to contain photographs of sensitive military installations and of the local submarine base. You believe that the holiday-maker is a spy, and you want to get him or her to confess.	You are a holidaymaker. You have been on holiday on this island, and you have taken lots of photos of the beach and the views of the sea from your hotel balcony. You just thought that they were nice views, and you knew nothing of the submarine base. You are an innocent holiday maker and not a spy.

Tableaux are frozen images, like freeze-frames from films, or still photographs, taken of a series of moments from a drama.

Improvisations are drama scenes where you make up your own words and movements as you go along.

Non-verbal communication is a way of conveying information without using words. For example, by hand movements or by the way someone holds their body.

What Where

BAM:	Well?
BOM:	[*Head bowed throughout.*] Nothing.
BAM:	He didn't say anything?
BOM:	No.
BAM:	You gave him the works?
BOM:	Yes.
BAM:	And he didn't say anything?
BOM:	No.
BAM:	He wept?
BOM:	Yes.
BAM:	Screamed?
BOM:	Yes.
BAM:	Begged for mercy?
BOM:	Yes.
BAM:	But didn't say anything?
BOM:	No.
V:	Not good.
	I start again.
BAM:	Well?
BOM:	Nothing.
BAM:	He didn't say it?
V*:	Good.
BOM:	No.
BAM:	You gave him the works?
BOM:	Yes.
BAM:	And he didn't say it?
BOM:	No.
BAM:	He wept?
BOM:	Yes.
BAM:	Screamed?
BOM:	Yes.

* V: this 'character' is a commentator or narrator

BAM:	Begged for mercy?
BOM:	Yes.
BAM:	But didn't say it?
BOM:	No.
BAM:	Then why stop?
BOM:	He passed out.
BAM:	And you didn't revive him?
BOM:	I tried.
BAM:	Well?
BOM:	I couldn't.
	[*Pause.*]
BAM:	It's a lie. [*Pause.*] He said it to you. [*Pause.*] Confess he said it to you. [*Pause.*] You'll be given the works until you confess.

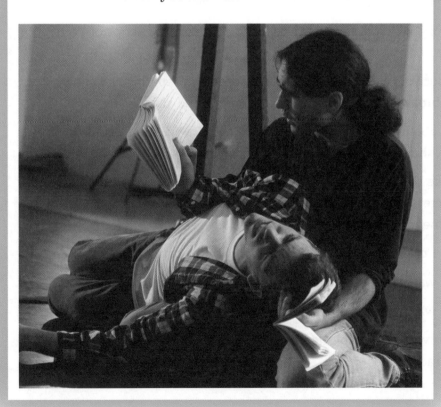

Reading for meaning

R 7
R 12

1 a) What themes is Beckett exploring in this play?

   b) What setting does the script suggest to you?

   c) Who are these characters and what might have happened?

2 Both *The Jewish Wife* and *What Where* portray characters who do not have much freedom. Identify three differences in the ways Brecht and Beckett present a similar idea. *Hint: Look at the setting, the non-verbal communication, the sentence structure, etc.*

3 Read *What Where* again and think carefully about the different status of the two main characters. Explain how Beckett makes the two characters different. Think about:

   • the differences in sentence lengths used by the two characters

   • the different sentence types used by the two characters

   • the way repetitions and pauses are used by the characters.

Drama

How might the scene from *What Where* be staged?

1 Working with a partner, read through and learn the script of *What Where*.

2 Test out your interpretations of the script by preparing and showing six **tableaux** from the scene to the rest of the class.

3 Think about the location of the scene and draw a stage plan from above, showing table, chairs and other props.

4 Practise the scene. Show the status relationship between the two characters and the atmosphere of the scene using voice and movement.

5 Make a critical evaluation of your work. Write paragraphs on:

   • the ways you used voice skills

   • the way you used movement skills

   • how well you established the differences between the two characters.

Writing to inform, explain and describe

With a partner, you are going to write a staging plan for *What Where* which two other students in your group can use to prepare a performance, and which you are going to present and justify to the rest of the class.

1 Take a clean copy of the script and, using a different coloured pen, write stage directions for how to **say** the lines. Include:

   - tone of voice

   - volume

   - pace

   - pausing.

2 Using a different coloured pen, write stage directions for the characters' **non-verbal communication** and **proxemics**.

3 Add advice about use of props and costume.

4 Draw your **set design**.

In drama, **proxemics** describe the spatial relations between characters and objects in a scene, such as how close one actor is to another.

The **set design** is the way a director or designer has arranged the stage. It includes the furniture and decoration.

Speaking and listening

S&L 2

1 a) Present the staging plan you prepared in *Writing to inform, explain and describe* to the class.

   b) After your presentation reflect on how well you got your ideas across, and how you could have improved your delivery.

2 Exchange staging plans with another pair. Follow their instructions to perform the scene in a different way.

3 Consider the different interpretations of the scene, evaluate them and decide which ideas are best.

Drama: script writing

1 As a class, discuss the topic of interrogation. Consider the differing viewpoints of the two main characters in *What Where*. How might they feel?

2 Working in pairs, script a continuation of the 'What Where' scene:

- begin by improvising as a pair
- polish your scene
- script it from the improvisation
- perform it together as a play.

3 Write an evaluation of all your performances in this section. Use the following paragraph prompts:

- describe what aspects of drama you have participated in
- evaluate your voice work in improvisation and scripted drama
- evaluate your movement work in improvisation and scripted drama
- evaluate your ability to stage script
- evaluate your ability to write script
- evaluate your ability to work as part of a group
- write a maximum of three targets for improvement of your drama work.

The power of speech

Queen Elizabeth's speech at Tilbury, 1588

In the sixteenth century there was enormous rivalry between England and Spain. King Philip II of Spain, a Roman Catholic, assembled a massive fleet of ships known as the Spanish Armada, and sailed them to England in an attempt to overthrow Elizabeth I, a Protestant.

At the battle off Gravelines on 29 July the English navy under Sir Francis Drake defeated the Armada. But in the Netherlands the Spanish army under the Duke of Parma was preparing to invade. There was no regular army in England. Men had been mustered to defend London and 4000 were assembled at Tilbury Fort in the Thames Estuary. There were real worries about the Queen's safety, but Elizabeth ignored her councillors' fears and determined to visit her troops. On 9 August, mounted on a horse and wearing a silver breastplate, she delivered this speech.

Before you read

R 2

1 Research Elizabeth I, using at least three different sources, such as:

- the Internet
- CD-ROM
- video
- television
- textbooks
- encyclopaedias.

Edit the material to produce a simple factfile.

2 Write a bibliography to show the different sources you have used. Include an evaluation of how useful each source was.

3 Discuss when it might be necessary for leaders to inspire their followers, as Elizabeth I does in the speech you are about to read.

As you read

- Think about the situation Elizabeth I is in as she sets about giving this rallying call to her people
- Notice the rhetorical devices she uses to appeal to her audience.

Queen Elizabeth's speech at Tilbury, 1588

My loving people, we have been persuaded by some, that are careful of our safety, to take heed how we commit ourselves to armed multitudes, for fear of treachery; but I assure you, I do not desire to live to distrust my faithful and loving people. Let tyrants fear; I have always so behaved myself that, under God, I have placed my chiefest strength and safeguard in the loyal hearts and good will of my subjects. And therefore I am come amongst you at this time, not as for my recreation or sport, but being resolved, in the midst and heat of the battle, to live or die amongst you all; to lay down, for my God, and for my kingdom, and for my people, my honour and my blood, even in the dust. I know I have but the body of a weak and feeble woman; but I have the heart of a king, and of a king of England, too; and think foul scorn that Parma or Spain, or any prince of Europe, should dare to invade the borders of my realms: to which, rather than any dishonour should grow by me, I myself will take up arms; I myself will be your general, judge, and rewarder of every one of your virtues in the field. I know already, by your forwardness, that you have deserved rewards and crowns; and we do assure you, on the word of a prince, they shall be duly paid you. In the mean my lieutenant general shall be in my stead, than whom never prince commanded a more noble and worthy subject; not doubting by your obedience to my general, by your concord in the camp, and by your valour in the field, we shall shortly have a famous victory over the enemies of my God, of my kingdom, and of my people.

R 12

Reading for meaning

1 This is a speech and Elizabeth spoke it out loud. In pairs, read it out loud in turn to make it as inspiring as possible.

2 Elizabeth starts by explaining that some advisers have tried to persuade her not to visit her troops at Tilbury.

   a) What does she give as their reason?

   b) What is her reason for going against their advice?

3 The speech is structured into three parts:

   * convincing the audience of the need to fight
   * explaining to the audience the Queen's own commitment to her country and the cause
   * promising to the audience that England will be victorious.

   Identify where each part begins and ends, and explain in your own words what Elizabeth says in each part.

4 Write out the entire first sentence of Elizabeth's speech.

   a) Underline all the **personal pronouns** and **possessive pronouns** she uses in this sentence. Why do you think she uses so many? Does she continue to use so many as the speech progresses?

   b) Circle the word Elizabeth repeats when describing her 'people' in this sentence. Why is she so careful to compliment them in this way?

   c) Find all the other compliments Elizabeth uses about her subjects/people in the speech, and make a list of the words.

   Personal pronouns are words used instead of the proper noun to classify people. For example: 'I', 'we', 'you', 'thou', 'he', 'she' and 'they' are personal pronouns. **Possessive pronouns** are words used to represent personal possession. For example: 'my', 'her', 'our' and 'his' are possessive pronouns.

5 Elizabeth is keen to point out that she has come to be 'amongst' her people. Write in your own words the reasons Elizabeth gives for going 'amongst' them. Think about the historical context and her gender when you answer this question.

6 Elizabeth repeats, 'my God', 'my kingdom' and 'my people', at various times in her speech. Why do you think these are so important for her to mention?

7 Analyse the **rhetorical devices** used by Elizabeth to inspire her subjects. Write a short paragraph for each device, support it with a quotation, and explain the effect of the device. You might include:

- use of pronouns
- complimenting the audience
- use of emotive language
- repetition.

Speaking and listening

1 In pairs, discuss how you would feel if you were in Elizabeth's audience. Inspired? Concerned? Patriotic? Say why.

2 Given the historical context of Elizabeth's speech, and the fact that she was a woman, do you find her speech remarkable?

3 How many people might have heard Elizabeth's speech? How would the speech have been reported and 'broadcast' among all her people?

Sentences

1 Read the speech again looking at the lengths of the sentences and the way they are extended by use of colons and semicolons. This is one way in which English has changed over time. Count the colons and semicolons in the sentence: 'I know I have but the … virtues in the field.'

2 Rewrite this sentence, taking out the colons and semicolons and making it into more than one sentence. This will give it a modern style. Use Elizabeth's words and standard English for the formal occasion.

3 How do your changes affect the meaning or power of Elizabeth's sentence?

The **colon** is a punctuation mark used to separate off examples, or lists, in order to allow a sentence to develop in a more complex way.

A **semicolon** is a punctuation mark that allows the writer to extend a sentence; it has a value between a comma and a full stop.

Churchill's speech after Dunkirk, June 4th 1940

At the end of May 1940, as a result of a skilfully organised retreat from the German army, the allied forces were evacuated from the beaches of Dunkirk. At first it was hoped that 45,000 men might be rescued, but in reality 338,000 allied troops reached England. On June 4th Churchill spoke to the House of Commons with the dual aim of celebrating the achievements of Dunkirk, and also of preparing the country for the challenges ahead. In the extracts you will read below, you will see that Winston Churchill set out to inspire his nation using similar rhetorical devices to those used by Queen Elizabeth I, almost four hundred years before.

Before you read

1 Research the sequence of events as they happened in 1940, leading up to the evacuation of forces from Dunkirk. Make a timeline leading up to Churchill's famous speech.

2 People often remember where they were and what they were doing at the time of great world events. Devise a series of simple questions and interview a friend or relative about their memories of Churchill.

As you read

• What effect is Churchill hoping to have on the people of Britain? What effect is he hoping to have on the people and leaders of other countries?

• Consider the range and size of the audience for Winston Churchill's speech, how it might be reported, and the means by which it would be broadcast around the world.

Extracts from Churchill's speech

Extract 1

The enemy attacked on all sides with great strength and fierceness, and their main power, the power of their far more numerous Air Force, was thrown into the battle or else concentrated upon Dunkirk and the beaches. Pressing in upon the narrow exit, both from the east and from the west, the enemy began to fire with cannon upon the beaches by which alone the shipping could approach or depart. They sowed magnetic mines in the channels and seas; they sent repeated waves of hostile aircraft, sometimes more than a hundred strong in one formation, to cast their bombs upon the single pier that remained, and upon the sand dunes upon which the troops had their eyes for shelter. Their U-boats, one of which was sunk, and their motor launches took their toll of the vast traffic which now began. For four or five days an intense struggle reigned. All their armoured divisions – or what was left of them – together with great masses of infantry and artillery, hurled themselves in vain upon the ever-narrowing, ever-contracting appendix within which the British and French Armies fought. **para 1**

Meanwhile, the Royal Navy, with the willing help of countless merchant seamen, strained every nerve to embark the British and Allied troops; 220 light warships and 650 other vessels were engaged. They had to operate upon the difficult coast, often in adverse weather, under an almost ceaseless hail of bombs and an increasing concentration of artillery fire. Nor were the seas, as I have said, themselves free from mines and torpedoes. It was in conditions such as these that our men carried on, with little or no rest, for days and nights on end, making trip after trip across the dangerous waters, bringing with them always men whom they had rescued. The numbers they have brought back are the measure of their devotion and their courage. The hospital ships, which brought off many thousands of British and French wounded, being so plainly marked were a special target for Nazi bombs; but the men and women on board them never faltered in their duty. **para 2**

Meanwhile, the Royal Air Force, which had already been
intervening in the battle, so far as its range would allow, from home
bases, now used part of its main metropolitan fighter strength, and
struck at the German bombers and at the fighters which in large
numbers protected them. This struggle was protracted and fierce.
Suddenly the scene has cleared, the crash and thunder has for the
moment – but only for the moment – died away. A miracle of
deliverance, achieved by valour, by perseverance, by perfect
discipline, by faultless service, by resource, by skill, by
unconquerable fidelity, is manifest to us all. The enemy was hurled
back by the retreating British and French troops. He was so
roughly handled that he did not hurry their departure seriously.
The Royal Air Force engaged the main strength of the German Air
Force, and inflicted upon them losses of at least four to one; and the
Navy, using nearly 1,000 ships of all kinds, carried over 335,000
men, French and British, out of the jaws of death and shame, to
their native land and to the tasks which lie immediately ahead. We
must be very careful not to assign to this deliverance the attributes
of a victory. Wars are not won by evacuations. But there was a
victory inside this deliverance, which should be noted. It was
gained by the Air Force. Many of our soldiers coming back have not
seen the Air Force at work; they saw only the bombers which
escaped its protective attack. They underrate its achievements. I
have heard much talk of this; that is why I go out of my way to say
this. I will tell you about it.

para 3

This was a great trial of strength between the British and German
Air Forces. Can you conceive a greater objective for the Germans in
the air than to make evacuation from these beaches impossible,
and to sink all these ships which were displayed, almost to the
extent of thousands? Could there have been an objective of greater
military importance and significance for the whole purpose of the

para 4

war than this? They tried hard, and they were beaten back; they were frustrated in their task. We got the Army away; and they have paid fourfold for any losses which they have inflicted. Very large formations of German aeroplanes – and we know that they are a very brave race – have turned on several occasions from the attack of one-quarter of their number of the Royal Air Force, and have dispersed in different directions. Twelve aeroplanes have been hunted by two. One aeroplane was driven into the water and cast away by the mere charge of a British aeroplane, which had no more ammunition. All of our types – the Hurricane, the Spitfire and the new Defiant – and all our pilots have been vindicated as superior to what they have at present to face.

When we consider how much greater would be our advantage in defending the air above this Island against an overseas attack, I must **para 5** say that I find in these facts a sure basis upon which practical and reassuring thoughts may rest. I will pay my tribute to these young airmen. The great French Army was very largely, for the time being, cast back and disturbed by the onrush of a few thousands of armoured vehicles. May it not also be that the cause of civilization itself will be defended by the skill and devotion of a few thousand airmen? There never has been, I suppose, in all the world, in all the history of war, such an opportunity for youth. The Knights of the Round Table, the Crusaders, all fall back into the past – not only distant but prosaic; these young men, going forth every morn to guard their native land and all that we stand for, holding in their hands these instruments of colossal and shattering power, of whom it may be said that

> Every morn brought forth a noble chance
> And every chance brought forth a noble knight,

deserve our gratitude, as do all the brave men who, in so many ways and on so many occasions, are ready, and continue ready to give life and all for their native land.

Extract 2

Turning once again, and this time more generally, to the question of invasion, I would observe that there has never been a period in all these long centuries of which we boast when an absolute guarantee against invasion, still less against serious raids, could have been given to our people. In the days of Napoleon the same wind which would have carried his transports across the Channel might have driven away the blockading fleet. There was always the chance, and it is that chance which has excited and befooled the imaginations of many Continental tyrants. Many are the tales that are told. We are assured that novel methods will be adopted, and when we see the originality of malice, the ingenuity of aggression, which our enemy displays, we may certainly prepare ourselves for every kind of novel stratagem and every kind of brutal and treacherous manoeuvre. I think that no idea is so outlandish that it should not be considered and viewed with a searching, but at the same time, I hope, with a steady eye. We must never forget the solid assurances of sea power and those which belong to air power if it can be locally exercised. *para 1*

I have, myself, full confidence that if all do their duty, if nothing is neglected, and if the best arrangements are made, as they are being made, we shall prove ourselves once again able to defend our Island home, to ride out the storm of war, and to outlive the menace of tyranny, if necessary for years, if necessary alone. At any rate, that is what we are going to try to do. That is the resolve of His Majesty's Government – every man of them. That is the will of Parliament and the nation. The British Empire and the French Republic, linked together in their cause and in their need, will defend to the death their native soil, aiding each other like good comrades to the utmost of their strength. Even though large tracts of Europe and many old and famous States have fallen or may fall into the grip of the Gestapo and all the odious apparatus of Nazi rule, we shall not flag or fail. We shall go on to the end, we shall fight in France, we shall fight on the seas and oceans, we shall fight with growing confidence and growing strength in the air, we shall defend our Island, whatever the cost may be, we shall fight on the beaches, we shall fight on the landing grounds, we shall fight in the fields and in the streets, we shall fight in the hills; we shall never surrender, and even if, which I do not for a moment believe, this *para 2*

Island or a large part of it were subjugated and starving, then our Empire beyond the seas, armed and guarded by the British Fleet, would carry on the struggle, until, in God's good time, the New World, with all its power and might, steps forth to the rescue and the liberation of the old.

Reading for meaning

W 7
R 12
S&L 7

1 Match the following summaries to the paragraphs in Churchill's speech:

a) we can take comfort from the valour of our young men – they will continue to defend us in the future

b) allied forces retreating from Dunkirk are attacked by the enemy

c) the Royal Navy aid embarkation and retreat, working in terrible conditions

d) strategic importance of this battle – German objective had been to prevent evacuation and sink ships

e) the Royal Airforce attack German bombers and fighters, forcing them back and allowing the evacuation to be successful

f) we must work together to overcome the threat

g) there is never a guarantee against a successful German invasion of Britain – we need to be prepared

2 How is the speech structured? Divide it into phases.

3 Winston Churchill singles out the actions of a number of groups of servicemen. Explain why he does this, and give examples from his speech to support your comments.

4 Winston Churchill uses strong language and colourful descriptions when speaking about Britain's enemies. Write down and explain some of the words and phrases used to describe the Nazis.

5 Identify different groups of people who would be listening to this speech. What is the intended effect Churchill wants to have on each group?

6 What **rhetorical devices** does Winston Churchill use to appeal to his audience?

Writing to compare

R 2
R 7

1 Reread the two speeches and look back at the paragraphs you wrote about Queen Elizabeth's use of **rhetorical devices**. Find similarities between the methods both leaders use to try to inspire and influence their audiences.

2 Collect your ideas in columns like the model below. Start with the same areas of **rhetorical device** that you used in your investigation of Elizabeth's speech, then add more.

Rhetorical devices	Elizabeth's speech	Winston Churchill's speech
Leaders use personal and possessive pronouns	'by **your** valour in the field, **we** shall shortly have a famous victory over the enemies of **my** God'	'**I** have, **myself**, full confidence that if all do their duty, if nothing is neglected, and if the best arrangements are made, we shall prove **ourselves**, once again able to defend our Island home.'

Wr 3

3 Write up your comparison as a piece of extended writing, using standard English.

- Write a paragraph for each area of comparison that you found.

- Link your sentences together by using connectives of comparison such as: *equally, in the same way, similarly, likewise, as with, like.*

- Include an example from each speech, in each paragraph.

- Finally explain why the leader has used this device.

A paragraph model might look like this:

In her speech Elizabeth compliments the courage and loyalty of her people, she says; they are 'faithful', and ' loving' and she calls the lieutenant general, 'noble', and 'worthy'. In the same way, Winston Churchill refers to the numbers rescued by the British as being: the measure of their devotion and their courage'.. Both leaders do this in order to show their respect for their people, and in order to make them feel unified by praising them.

You should take about 30 minutes to write up your answer.

Wr14

Writing to inform, explain and describe

In order to unify their own people behind their cause, both leaders need to provide a negatively biased impression of their enemy.

Imagine you are a Spanish spy; you have listened to Elizabeth's speech and you write a letter to the Duke of Parma. Try to create an account that is biased against Elizabeth, and which is positive about the chances of the Spanish army.

Writing to persuade, argue and advise

Sn 3

1 Imagine you are the coach of the year 9 school sports team. Your team is in the final of the 'Schools Cup' (for whatever sport you like!).

   a) Write a rousing speech in formal standard English that you could deliver just before the match to the team and its supporters.

   • Think of ways to appeal to your audience, to inspire them to do well.

   • Use the **rhetorical devices** Queen Elizabeth and Winston Churchill use in their speeches.

   b) Evaluate the quality of your speech. Perform it to the class. Include both *how* you delivered your speech, and what the content was like.

2 Imagine it is half time in the final of the sports event and your team is losing. Invent a less formal speech to encourage them to improve in the second half. Use language to suit your purpose.

From prose to drama

Metamorphosis by Franz Kafka

The short story 'Metamorphosis', which recounts the transformation of the young travelling salesman Gregor Samsa into a dung beetle, was written by the Czech writer Franz Kafka in 1912.

S&L 2

R 2

Before you read

1   What stories, cartoons or films do you know in which animals behave like human beings, or in which humans are transformed into animals?

2   Use an encyclopaedia and the Internet to find out about **dung beetles**.

  • What do dung beetles eat?

  • What is their natural habitat?

  • How do they move?

  • What distinguishing features and characteristics do they possess?

3   Why do you think Kafka chose to transform his human character into a dung beetle? Explain your theory.

As you read

Think about:

• what Gregor is feeling and what he is trying to do during this extract.

• what his daily routine as a travelling salesman is usually like.

METAMORPHOSIS

I

As Gregor Samsa awoke one morning from uneasy dreams he found himself transformed in his bed into a gigantic insect. He was lying on his hard, as it were armour-plated, back and when he lifted his head a little he could see his domelike brown belly divided into stiff arched segments on top of which the bed quilt could hardly stay in place and was about to slide off completely. His numerous legs, which were pitifully thin compared to the rest of his bulk, waved helplessly before his eyes.

What has happened to me? he thought. It was no dream. His room, a regular human bedroom, only rather too small, lay quiet within its four familiar walls. Above the table on which a collection of cloth samples was unpacked and spread out – Samsa was a travelling salesman – hung the picture which he had recently cut out of an illustrated magazine and put into a pretty gilt frame. It showed a lady, with a fur hat on and a fur stole, sitting upright and holding out to the spectator a huge fur muff into which the whole of her forearm had vanished!

Gregor's eyes turned next to the window, and the overcast sky – one could hear raindrops beating on the window gutter – made him quite melancholy. What about sleeping a little longer and forgetting all this nonsense, he thought, but it could not be done, for he was accustomed to sleep on his right side and in his present condition he could not turn himself over. However violently he forced himself towards his right side he always rolled onto his back again. He tried it at least a hundred times, shutting his eyes to keep from seeing his struggling legs, and only desisted when he began to feel in his side a faint dull ache he had never felt before.

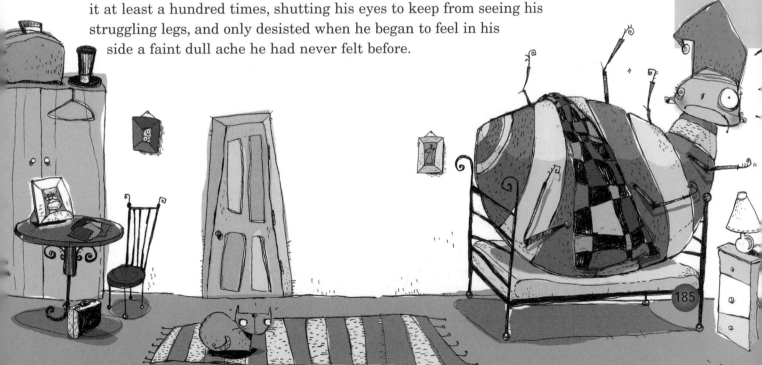

Oh God, he thought, what an exhausting job I've picked out for myself! On the road day in, day out. It's much more irritating work than doing the actual business in the home office, and on top of that there's the trouble of constant travelling, of worrying about train connections, the bad food and irregular meals, casual acquaintances that are always new and never become intimate friends. The devil take it all! He felt a slight itching up on his belly, slowly pushed himself on his back nearer to the top of the bed so that he could lift his head more easily, identified the itching place which was surrounded by many small white spots the nature of which he could not understand and was about to touch it with a leg, but drew the leg back immediately, for the contact made a cold shiver run through him.

He slid down again into his former position. This getting up early, he thought, can make an idiot out of anyone. A man needs his sleep. Other salesmen live like harem women. For instance, when I come back to the hotel in the morning to write up my orders these others are only sitting down to breakfast. Let me just try that with my boss; I'd be fired on the spot. Anyhow, that might be quite a good thing for me, who can tell? If I didn't have to hold back because of my parents I'd have given notice long ago, I'd have gone to the boss and told him exactly what I think of him. That would knock him right off his desk! It's a peculiar habit of his, too, sitting on top of the desk like that and talking down to employees, especially when they have to come quite near because the boss is hard of hearing. Well, there's still hope; once I've saved enough money to pay back my parents' debts to him – that should take another five or six years – I'll do it without fail. I'll cut my ties completely then. For the moment, though, I'd better get up, since my train leaves at five.

He looked at the alarm clock ticking on the chest of drawers. Heavenly Father! he thought. It was half-past six and the hands were quietly moving on, it was even past the half-hour, it was getting on toward a quarter to seven. Had the alarm clock not gone off? From the bed one could see that it had been properly set for four o'clock; of course it must have gone off. Yes, but was it possible to sleep quietly through that ear-splitting noise? Well, he had not slept quietly, yet apparently all the more soundly for that. But what was he to do now? The next train went at seven o'clock; to catch that he would need to hurry like mad and his samples weren't even packed, and he himself wasn't feeling

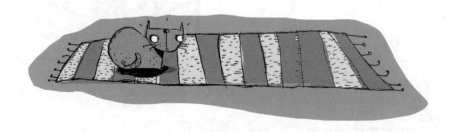

particularly fresh and energetic. And even if he did catch the train he couldn't avoid a tirade from the boss, since the messenger boy must have been waiting for the five o'clock train and must have long since reported his failure to turn up. This messenger was a creature of the boss's, spineless and stupid. Well, supposing he were to say he was sick? But that would be very awkward and would look suspicious, since during his five years' employment he had not been ill once. The boss himself would be sure to come with the health insurance doctor, would reproach his parents for their son's laziness, and would cut all excuses short by handing the matter over to the insurance doctor, who of course regarded all mankind as perfectly healthy malingerers. And would he be so far wrong in this case? Gregor really felt quite well, apart from a drowsiness that was quite inexcusable after such a long sleep, and he was even unusually hungry.

As all this was running through his mind at top speed without his being able to decide to leave his bed – the alarm clock had just struck a quarter to seven – there was a cautious tap at the door near the head of his bed. 'Gregor,' said a voice – it was his mother's – 'it's a quarter to seven. Didn't you have a train to catch?' That gentle voice! Gregor had a shock as he heard his own voice answering hers, unmistakably his own voice, it was true, but with a persistent horrible twittering squeak behind it like an undertone, which left the words in their clear shape only for the first moment and then rose up reverberating around them to destroy their sense, so that one could not be sure one had heard them rightly. Gregor wanted to answer at length and explain everything, but in the circumstances he confined himself to saying: 'Yes, yes, thank you, Mother, I'm getting up now.' The wooden door between them must have kept the change in his voice from being noticeable outside, for his mother contented herself with this statement and shuffled away. Yet this brief exchange of words had made the other members of the family aware that Gregor was, strangely, still at home, and at one of the side doors his father was already knocking, gently, yet with his fist. 'Gregor, Gregor,' he called. 'What's the matter with you?' And after a little while he called again in a deeper voice: 'Gregor! Gregor!' At the other side door his sister was saying in a low, plaintive tone: 'Gregor? Aren't you well? Do you need anything?'

Reading for meaning

1 Gregor is a travelling salesman, and the main breadwinner for his family. His life is clearly a difficult one. Write a list of all the pressures he is under.

2 How would you describe Gregor's reactions to his new situation?

3 Gregor's transformation into a dung beetle can be seen as a metaphor for his troubled existence. Explain why Kafka chooses a beetle, and what you think he is trying to tell us about the society Gregor lives in.

4 Kafka structures his writing carefully to blend his narrative account of the morning with descriptions of what Gregor looks like as an insect, and how he moves. Write a fully detailed description of the insect-Gregor's appearance, and his movements.

5 Kafka makes Gregor's experience seem horrifying. We find out a lot about Gregor, and we sympathise with him.

a) From whose point of view is the story written?

b) What is the atmosphere or mood of the story like?

c) How does Kafka structure the narrative to inform us about the past and the present of Gregor's life?

Sentences

1 There are three sentences in the opening paragraph of the story. What facts are conveyed by each sentence?

2 Why does Kafka choose to put the sentences in the order that he does?

3 Rewrite the opening paragraph of 'Metamorphosis', changing the order in which Kafka presents the information.

Try keeping the phrase: 'he found himself transformed in his bed into a gigantic insect', until the third sentence of the paragraph.

4 What effect does changing the order of the information presented in the first paragraph have on the start of the story? Which order is more effective and why? Use quotations from the text to support your answer.

Metamorphosis by Steven Berkoff

In the late 1960s, the playwright Steven Berkoff was inspired to transform Kafka's story of Gregor from prose to drama. As well as rewriting 'Metamorphosis' as a play, Berkoff directed and acted in the first production, taking on the role of Gregor.

Before you read

You have read the opening of Kafka's story, 'Metamorphosis'. Imagine you have been asked to turn it into a play.

• What sorts of things would you need to bear in mind?

• What are the main differences between the way a story is written and the way a play appears on the page?

As you read

1   Think about what the play would look like and sound like in performance. Using the stage directions to help you, write notes quickly in bullet point form on:

• the movements you would see

• the light and sound effects there would be.

Use the table below as a guide. Give line references.

Line ref.	Movements	Line ref.	Light or sound effects
6	Family form beetle and wave arms in a line	7	Family lit up at the front of the stage

 2   Working in groups of four, take parts and read the opening of the play together.

Metamorphosis

The FAMILY enters one at a time – backcloth lit – figures appear in silhouette. Each one enters in the character he or she is going to play, and performs a small mime condensing the personality into a few seconds. MOTHER is first – describes a sad face – leaves a pained heart and angst. FATHER next strolls boldly on in boots and costume of mid-European lower middle-class tradesman – trousers in socks – braces – no jacket, looking like Hindenburg. Then GRETA, as a student with violin. Then GREGOR, who just walks on and smiles – an amiable being.

As each speaks they form a line behind each other. On the last line they take on the movement of an insect by moving their arms to a particular rhythm. As no front lighting is used, this has the effect of an insect's leg movements.

MR S: [*enters*] As Gregor Samsa awoke one morning from uneasy
dreams …

MRS S: [*enters*] He found himself transformed in his bed into a
gigantic insect …

GRETA: [*enters*] His numerous legs, which were pitifully thin   5
compared to the rest of his bulk, waved helplessly before him.

[*Movement starts.* GREGOR *is in front. Suddenly the movement stops – * FAMILY *dissolve the beetle image by moving away – leaving* GREGOR *still moving as part of the insect image.*] [*Front lights come up revealing* FAMILY.]

GREGOR: What has happened to me?

FAMILY: He thought.

GREGOR: It was no dream.

GRETA: He looked at the alarm clock ticking on the chest. 10

GREGOR: Half past six and the hands were quietly moving on.

MR S: Said a voice.

GREGOR: That gentle voice…

GRETA: It was his mother's…

MR S: His mother's… 15

MRS S: His mother's…

[*Fade.*] [*Slow Tick*] [*Lights snap up on the centre area downstage revealing* GREGOR *standing behind* GRETA *– scenes of pre-insect life. Each speak their own thoughts which run contrapuntally.*]

GREGOR: [*indicates*] I'm Gregor Samsa – there's my sister Greta.

GRETA: [*motionless*] There's brother Gregor.

GREGOR: Isn't that nice that she waits up for me.

GRETA: I always wait up for him. 20

GREGOR: Glass of milk on the table then bed – up again at four a.m. Yes, four a.m.! To catch the five a.m. train.

GRETA: He doesn't come home often.

GREGOR: Daily! What a life – what an exhausting job, and I picked it.

GRETA: He works so hard. 25

GREGOR: I picked it? I'm a commercial traveller in the cloth trade – I have to work to keep them.

[*Lights snap on downstage left and right revealing* MOTHER *and* FATHER *both frozen.*]

GRETA: But he also makes things at home.

GREGOR: Who else can do it? Father's ill so they rely on me totally.

GRETA: He recently made a picture frame and in it he put a picture 30 cut out of an illustrated magazine.

GREGOR: On my back it rests – their fortunes rest on my back like a great weight.

GRETA: It shows a lady with a fur cap and fur stole sitting upright and holding out to the spectator a huge fur muff into which 35 the whole of her forearm had vanished.

[*Image of above – music.*]

GREGOR: The warehouse was better – one didn't have to worry about the travelling.

GRETA: It was very good.

GREGOR: I feel sick.   40

   [*Dissolve.*] [*A loud ticking is heard which continues throughout the next scene – GREGOR marches behind his FAMILY who in time to the ticking call out GREGOR's meaning for them. Double time for GREGOR going about his work.*]

GRETA: Gregor!

MR S: Cash!

GRETA: Gregor!

MR S: Shoes!

GRETA: Gregor!   45

MR S: Cigars!

GRETA: Gregor!

MRS S: Food!

GRETA: Gregor!

MR S: Beef!   50

GRETA: Gregor!

MRS S: Clothes!

   [*As GREGOR comes to stop behind GRETA – FAMILY mime actions of domestic life in time to ticking resembling those automatic figures in waxworks – they repeat same combinations of gestures – only when they speak do they freeze the movement.*]

GRETA: Milk, Gregor?

   [*Image – actors as marionettes. FATHER smokes cigar and drinks. MOTHER sews. GRETA reads her school books.*]

GREGOR: Thanks – you're up late, why aren't you in bed?

GRETA: I thought I'd wait up for you. What's the matter?   55

GREGOR: My back's aching – must be carrying these samples all day.

   [*Freeze action during next five speeches.*]

MR S: Did you sell much?

GREGOR: Not as much as last week.

MR S: [*disappointed*] Oh! – never mind – it'll be better tomorrow.

GREGOR: Perhaps.   60

MR S: Of course it will.   [*Continue action.*]

GREGOR: Ssh …listen …

GRETA: What?

GREGOR: It's raining again – hear it beating on the window gutter?

MRS S: [*listening*] It's been raining for ages.   65

GREGOR: Oh God! [*Sits down wearily.*]

GRETA: What is it?

GREGOR: I'm so exhausted.

MR S: Go to bed then.

Reading for meaning

1 How does Berkoff create the character of the insect for the reader? *Hint: Consider directions, choreographed movements, sounds and voices, and the way the whole family is integrated into the action.*

2 How does Berkoff create an atmosphere of stress and pressure for Gregor? *Hint: Consider sound effects, like the clock ticking, and the sound of the rainfall, and the voices of the family calling out what they want from Gregor.*

Writing to compare

R K
W 3
R 7

Write a comparison of the differences and similarities between Kafka's 'Metamorphosis' and Berkoff's *Metamorphosis*. Explain which you prefer, and give reasons for your opinions.

- Link your comments with connectives of comparison like 'similarly', 'in the same way'; and of contrast like 'on the other hand', 'whereas'.

- Use the following paragraph topics:

  – the presentation of the character of Gregor

  – the presentation of the insect

  – the presentation of the family

  – the creation of atmosphere

  – the differences in sentence structure and layout

  – which version you like best and why.

- Write in standard English and check the accuracy of your spelling and punctuation.

- Take 35 minutes to write up your comparison.

Writing to persuade, argue and advise

You are going to write two letters, one from a doctor and one, in reply, from a member of Gregor's family.

1   You are a doctor who has examined Gregor. You have decided that it would be best for all concerned if Gregor were 'put to sleep'. Write a letter to the Samsa family arguing that in this case, euthanasia would be the best course of action. As a doctor, you should use a professional and impersonal tone.

2   You are Mrs Samsa. Write a reply to the doctor's letter arguing that regardless of Gregor's appearance, and regardless of the severity of his needs, you intend to keep him because he is still part of your family. Answer each of the doctor's points, with solutions, and produce a counter-argument trying to find weaknesses in the doctor's point of view.

In both letters you could use some of the following techniques to help your argument:

- statistics
- quotations from experts
- emotive language
- exaggeration
- personal anecdotes
- a strong voice.

Wr 5

Writing to imagine, explore and entertain

1   Write your own prose opening to a metamorphosis story about the pressures facing a modern teenager. Begin your story:

   As .... awoke one morning from troubled dreams (s)he found (her)himself transformed in (her) his bed into a ....

   Structure the story in the same way as Kafka.

2   Now, following Berkoff's format, rewrite the beginning of your own story as the opening to a play.

   • Involve the family in order to make extra characters.

   • Add stage directions to create action, movements and mime.

   • Add sound effects to create atmosphere.

Review

With a partner, explore what you have learned in this chapter.

1 Choose:
- your best piece of work
- your least successful piece of work.

2 Read or allow your partner to read each piece of work. Explain to your partner the reasons for your choice. Identify features which you:
- used successfully
- need to develop.

Focus on comparing texts

Individually, look at the work you have done on comparing different texts (page 182 and page 193).

1 What did you find most difficult about these activities?

2 What technique helped you most in the preparation stage?

3 How well did you use connectives?

4 To what extent did you use quotations or reference to text?

5 What was successful about your finished piece of work?

6 What could you improve in your next comparative piece?

List three techniques you will need to remember for your end of Key Stage assessment.

Set up to three targets for improving your next piece of work. You might set targets such as:

a) use quotation more frequently

b) structure my arguments/ideas more logically

c) take notes as I read the text.

The Reading test

Preparing for Assessment Focus 6

Assessment Focus 6: identify and comment on writers' purposes and viewpoints, and the effect of the text on the reader.

This assessment focus asks you to recognise that behind every text there is a writer who chooses the content and style of their writing to create a specific effect on the reader. The questions will often ask you to explain 'how', 'why' and 'what effect'. The 'reader' may also be referred to as 'we' or 'us'. If you are required to say how *you* respond as a reader, you must base your comments on evidence from the text. Some texts are addressed to a particular reader. For example: letters, leaflets, texts from a different culture or time. In these cases, you might need to imagine you are the actual reader for whom the text was written. If the text is a speech or play, imagine you are the listener or audience instead of 'reader'.

Example

The following sample questions are based on 'The Jewish Wife' by Brecht on pages 156–158.

1a) **This play was written as a criticism of Nazi policies. Find evidence for the following purposes: (1 mark for each)**

- **To show the effect of the new laws on the lives of individuals**
  'I'm packing so they shan't take away your job as a senior physician'

- **To describe the Nazi leaders in critical terms**
  'liars'

Examiner's comments

The quotations from the monologue illustrate the stated purposes of the text and 1 mark is gained for each, giving a total of 2 marks. For the first purpose 'they've stopped saying good morning to you at the clinic' and 'you're not sleeping nowadays' could have been chosen instead as evidence that the wife has to leave. For the second purpose, alternative quotations would have been 'semi-barbarians' or 'monsters'.

b) **Give another purpose of the text. (1 mark)**
- To criticise ordinary people who don't speak out against Nazis.

Examiner's comments

I mark was awarded. Brecht does intend influencing opinions and encouraging people not to just agree with what is happening. Other possible purposes could have been chosen.

2   What is the effect on the audience of hearing the woman's thoughts before her conversation with her husband? (5 marks)

As we watch the duologue, we adopt the point of view of the woman because we know more about her feelings from the monologue, so we sympathise with her more. We feel sorry for her because we know the dilemma she is in. She has had to accept the reality: 'And you aren't to pretend it's just a matter of four weeks either.' Without the monologue, we would have interpreted her character differently. We might think she doesn't realise it won't be for just a short time. We also wonder how we might react in her situation.

Some people in the audience might not agree with the attitude she takes, thinking that she has to uproot herself to allow her husband to have a better life. They might hope her husband wouldn't allow it to happen and would be disappointed that he seems so weak in the duologue: 'It might not be such a bad idea, I suppose'. The information we are given in the monologue helps us to realise that the husband is naïve or even untruthful. When he says he'll 'see they give me a special permit' to send her some money, he sounds authoritative, but we already know it won't be possible and that he knows this: 'And don't tell me you'll send me money; you know you won't be allowed to.'

Also, the monologue where she rehearses what she might say to him led us to believe she was going to have the courage to speak openly to him and explain her feelings. The audience would feel frustrated that the woman doesn't say what she really thinks. When she says she is packing because 'I want to get away', we know she is really going because she felt she had to for her husband's sake. The audience might wish that they could tell the husband the truth themselves! For each response that she makes, we recall what she had actually rehearsed and what she should have said in reply.

Examiner's comments

This response makes good use of the text to support each point. Sufficient different reasons are given to merit the award of the full 5 marks: the sympathy, the way our knowledge allows us to adopt the wife's point of view and the frustration that she doesn't tell the husband openly how she feels. There is appropriate focus on the impact of the monologue on the audience listening to the duologue and how the audience links the two directly in their mind.

Practice

1   **What does the monologue tell us about Brecht's view of Jews? (5 marks)**

2   **How would the audience of the time have felt during the monologue?**

The Writing test

Writing to imagine, explore and entertain

Example

Imagine an incident where someone is discriminated against or treated unfairly.
Write the story of what happens and how they feel. (30 marks)
• **Make your reader feel sympathy for your character.**

Examiner's comments

The main task is given in **bold** *print and is introduced by some information that will help you to respond. In this example, there is no specific information about the* **audience** *for your writing so assume it is the general reader. The* **purpose** *of the writing is to entertain and/or to sympathise; you are told the type of writing (a story) and are given some ideas about* **content** *(what happened/how they feel).*

Planning

Before you start writing your response, you should spend a few minutes noting down some key points and deciding how you will organise them. Good answers explore the issues in detail and are clearly organised.

Content

For your story you should:

• explain the incident

• show what your characters are like and how they feel, through description, dialogue and action.

Organisation and style

• You could write a third-person narrative, or tell the story from the point of view of one (or more) of the characters.

• You could tell the story in chronological order, or reveal what happened in a different order. You don't have to start at the beginning!

A story is **narrative** writing. You will need to use the features of this text type:
• usually first- or third-person narrative
• different sentence structures are chosen to create atmosphere
• vocabulary is chosen to reveal character and to create atmosphere
• the visual and sound effects of language might be used. For example: imagery, alliteration, onomatopoeia, rhyme, rhythm.

Here is part of a story written by a student in response to this task. Look at the features of narrative writing that have been used.

Neil: Let me tell you about my new bedroom. It is huge! I've got a TV, a DVD player, a computer and a games cube. There's plenty of room for all my skateboard gear, too. I'm so looking forward to my birthday because Dad said I could have all of my friends round. I know they'll be impressed.

Darren: So, this is where I'm going to be living. I don't mind Mum re-marrying and I know we had to have somewhere to go, but it's just who she re-married that bothers me. I don't like Neil, either. I did try at first but they both treat me like I don't exist. Neil grabbed the biggest room as soon as we saw the house but when I tried to argue, Mum just gave me one of her looks and I knew, immediately, that I needn't waste the effort. Why doesn't she just stick up for me sometimes? Neil always gets his own way. It is like Mum doesn't want to upset Mike. Even the baby has got a bigger room than me. I wonder whether Neil thinks it is strange, me calling his Dad 'Mike'. I know every time Neil calls Mum 'Maureen', it reminds me that he didn't used to be part of our family. I wish I could go and stay with Dad. At least it would just be us, then.

Examiner's comments

This is a first-person dual narrative, taking the point of view of both characters. The language has a spoken feel to it. Darren asks more questions (rhetorical questions) than Neil, suggesting that he is more reflective and analytical. It goes straight into the events, so we don't yet know the background. This begins to be revealed: 'new' bedroom; birthday; remarriage – are they stepbrothers now? We also begin to learn about the characters. Neil tells us about himself and doesn't mention Darren, suggesting that he is not important. Neil is portrayed as being popular ('all of my friends'), spoilt ('I've got a ... and ...') and a show-off ('I know they'll be impressed'). The exclamation mark after 'huge!' indicates the emphasis he puts on the size of the room. Darren, on the other hand, tells us about other people: we learn of his relationship with Mike, his mum ('gave me one of her looks and I knew ...') and their relationship with each other ('It is like Mum doesn't want to upset Mike.'). He seems more sensitive, experiencing the strangeness of having a stepdad. When he uses the word 'grabbed' to describe the way Neil chose his room, it reveals how Darren feels about Neil: he takes things for himself, doesn't share with others, is quick to find what he wants and to look after himself. At the start, Darren seems resigned to his 'fate': 'So, this is where I'm going to be living.'

Practice

Now write your own response to this task.

5

Media

Preparation for GCSE

This chapter looks at two media: television and the Internet. You will study different types of reality TV shows and investigate the different attitudes towards them and the ethical nature of these types of programme.

You will also study the Internet and the way information is presented. Specifically, you will study the websites for two young people's television channels and you will analyse the sites in terms of their content and style.

This chapter will prepare you for your GCSE coursework. Each section will end with a coursework question for you to prepare.

TRUMAN HOUS

5.1 Reality TV

Big Brother

'Big Brother' is a British reality TV programme in which contestants are installed in a house and filmed 'secretly' as they live there. Over the weeks, the television viewers and the contestants themselves vote to eject or retain fellow contestants until the house contains one occupant only – the winner.

You are going to read an extract from the fourth series of Big Brother in which two of the contestants are talking. The conversation started when Jade asked Spencer what he did for a living.

Before you read

1 Write a list of everything you did on one day last weekend. Include conversations you had and places you went. It is important to record this honestly, including bad-tempered outbursts, lazing in front of the TV, and refusing to tidy your bedroom.

2 Now imagine a reality TV producer who wants:

   • to get positive audience response to you

   • to get negative audience response to you.

   Create two separate storyboards of the events and conversations that took place. Write captions for each.

3 How did you generate the different responses? What does this tell you about reality television?

Jade Goody

Spencer: 'You know you see those people in Venice standing on the back of gondolas, pushing it around?'

Jade: 'They don't do that on the Thames though, do they?'

Spencer: 'No. I don't work on the Thames. I work in Cambridge.'

Jade: 'Is there not the Thames there?'

Spencer: 'No!'

Jade: 'Is there a river called the Cambridge river?'

Spencer: 'Yeah, it's called the Cam.'

Jade: 'Really? You swear? I only thought there was the Thames. I thought that was the main one in London.'

Spencer: 'It is. I don't live in London.'

Jade: 'I'm confused. I thought Cambridge was in London. I knew Birmingham weren't in London.'

Spencer: 'Would you like to go and tell the group what you just said?'

Jade: 'No ...'

Spencer: 'Cambridge is a city.'

Jade: 'But we've got a city in London.'

Spencer: 'Yes. This city is called London. And there's different parts of it. Cambridge is a city.'

Jade: 'Of where? Kent?

Jade:	'Well England's a country, London's a city, Bermondsey's just a throw-off. Now where are you? What's your country, and what's your things?'
Spencer:	'What country am I from? England. The city is called Cambridge, the county Cambridgeshire.'
Jade:	'So not Kent then?'
Spencer:	'Nooooo ... The region is called East Anglia.'
Jade:	'East Angular? That's abroad. Is there not a place called East Angular abroad?'
Spencer:	'Jade, have you been taking the stupid pills again?'
Jade:	'Every time people tell me they work in East Angular, I actually think they're talking about near Tunisia and places like that. Am I thick?'
Spencer:	'Well, I hate to say it, but you are.'
Jade:	'Cos Scottish and Irish and all that comes under England, doesn't it?'
Spencer:	'No ... They come under Great Britain. Scotland and Wales have their own flags. Northern Ireland and Ireland are different.'
Jade:	'So they're not together? Where's Berlin?'
Spencer:	'Germany...'

Reading for meaning

1. What do you learn about Jade and Spencer from this extract?

2. How do you respond to the two characters?

3. Why do you think these two people were selected as contestants for Big Brother?

Public Enemy Number 1

'Public Enemy Number 1' is an article taken from a tabloid newspaper about the behaviour of Jade Goody, the contestant from the extract on page 205–207.

Public Enemy Number 1

By Mel Hunter

Two-faced Jade Goody may be having a hard time inside the Big Brother house but that's nothing compared with the hassle she will get outside. Like Nasty Nick before her, dimwit Jade is fast becoming one of the most hated people in Britain. During her five weeks in the house, the 21-year-old dental nurse has found only one thing she is good at – stabbing her housemates in the back.

The Sun revealed last week how Jade had been ordered to see the show psychotherapist in the diary room after viewers complained about her bitching. The show's bosses feared angry viewers would make Jade's life hell unless she cleaned up her act. After the session with the shrink Jade vowed to change and started by apologising to Sophie.

But viewers are unlikely to be fooled. They have had enough of Jade's boozing and bitching.

Nasty Nick Bateman says Jade will be in for a surprise. He said: 'She will get a tough time from the Press and the public but at the end of the day she has been warned.' Nick said if Jade wanted advice from him, all she had to do was call.

However, The Sun's agony aunt Deirdre Sanders says we should not be too quick to judge Jade. Deirdre said: 'She is a product of her upbringing.'

That upbringing includes a difficult childhood in Bermondsey, South London. Her parents split up when she was a toddler. Mum Jacqueline lost the use of her arm in a motorcycle accident and her dad is in jail.

Jade herself admitted to being caught shoplifting in the exclusive London department store Selfridges.

Deirdre said: 'She is a girl who has had quite a tough life so we should not be completely down on her.' Deirdre believes Jade will need massive emotional support to help her ride out the abuse she gets after leaving the house. But Jade does have her strengths, says Deirdre, and she must draw on those if she is to rebuild her life after Big Brother. 'She is entertaining and bubbly and can make people feel good about themselves. What she hasn't got is consistency. She is not good at sustaining relationships because she didn't have that as she was growing up.'

The same behaviour landed Nasty Nick in hot water after he left the house during the show's first series two years ago. He was subjected to months of abuse and told The Sun how his dramatic exit had left him fearing the future. He said he lived in fear of being beaten up. Unless Jade has a dramatic personality change, there are fears she may suffer the same fate. Jade looks set to be evicted this week, after apparently being nominated for eviction by her housemates.

Jade has already had a taste of things to come when she leaves the Big Brother house. She overheard chants of 'Get Jade Out' on the night Sophie was evicted last week. She urged fellow housemates to listen to the crowd and said: 'Can you hear that? They want me out.'

Evicted housemate Lee Davey told The Sun Jade – dubbed Miss Piggy – would have a tough time when she comes out.

He said: 'Every time I go out people ask me what it was like with Jade. They want to climb over the fence and punch her. There will be a lot of boos when she comes out – and I'll be leading them. She's an idiot and I will have no sympathy for her when she comes out.'

Deirdre warns that Jade will feel the emotional 'come down' on the outside much harder than most. But a spokesman for Big Brother insisted that Jade was tough enough to cope with whatever came her way.

He says: 'They all get a big talk before they go into the house to prepare them for an intense experience and they are warned that this could be a really bad time. It is called the 'talk of doom' and it is basically to put them off and warn them of the possible consequences – and to check they are tough enough to cope whatever the outcome. We have strong aftercare for contestants and their families. We won't abandon her.'

But even the headteacher of Jade's old school is worried about his former pupil. Tony Perry is principal of Bacon's College where Jade spent her formative years. The school has been blasted for giving dimwit Jade a poor education but Bacon's College in Rotherhithe, south-east London, is in fact one of Britain's best state schools. Last year it had a 72% GCSE pass rate at grades A to C. Mr Perry said: 'We did try our best for her, as we do for all our pupils.'

Yet for all the bad press which Jade may have brought Bacon's College, the school's headteacher has nothing but sympathy for his former pupil. He told The Sun: 'I feel very uncomfortable about a young person being put in the artificial goldfish bowl of Big Brother. I think it very cynical and very exploitative. And I am worried about what will become of Jade after the experience.'

Aren't we all, Mr Perry. Aren't we all.

Reading for meaning

1 List the specific examples of Jade's behaviour in the house mentioned in the article that have earned her the title of 'Public Enemy Number 1'.

2 Identify five comments that are fact and five that are opinions from the article.

3 Using evidence from the article, explain why agony aunt Deirdre Sanders thinks we should not be too judgemental of Jade's behaviour.

4 Quotation from experts or witnesses is a common feature of informative or persuasive writing. It is used to give extra value.

Using a table like the one below, record the quotes in the article regarding Jade and her behaviour. Make a note of who said the quote, what their role is and what they said.

Name	Role	Quote
Lee Davey	Former housemate	'Every time I go out people ask me what it was like with Jade. They want to climb over the fence and punch her. There will be a lot of boos when she comes out – and I'll be leading them.'

5 What impressions does the article give of Jade's former school, Bacon's College?

6 This article is taken from *The Sun*, a tabloid newspaper.

a) What are the features of this type of journalism?

b) What features identify this as a tabloid article?

Vocabulary

1 a) Pick out adjectives and phrases used to describe Jade in the article.

   b) Organise them into two groups: positive and negative.

2 What do you notice about the way Jade is described?

Research

Find out as much information as you can about 'Big Brother'. As part of your research you should examine:

- the layout of the Big Brother house
- the format of the show and the rules of the house
- the target audience
- how to apply and the auditions
- the showing times and different types of programme broadcast, the channels it is shown on, other media used to broadcast 'Big Brother' or information about 'Big Brother'
- how the show is used for marketing and commercial purposes.

Writing to imagine, explore and entertain

Imagine you have just been evicted from the Big Brother house. Describe leaving the Big Brother house in as much detail as possible. In your description you should include:

- whether you were the first person to be evicted, the last but one or somewhere in the middle
- why you think you were evicted
- how the audience and crowds respond to your eviction
- what you enjoyed or hated about being in the house
- what you think about your former housemates.

Experiment with sentences and tenses to exaggerate the immediacy of the experience of being evicted.

We wouldn't put mice through this

Reality TV producers forget that their participants are human

For a medium which once justified itself by claiming a mission to educate, television can be horribly slow to learn. In the recent past, an American game show called Who Wants to Marry a Millionaire? – in which a guy claimed as his prize a bride he'd never met – rapidly collapsed into divorce, litigation and scandal. Even more recently, a couple launched a lawsuit after returning to find a corpse in their hotel room, left there, it turned out, by a 'prank' TV show.

Other professions would see warnings here. But TV often seems to be like a driver who speeds up after passing paramedics dragging bodies from a car crash. ITV1 is reported to be piloting a gameshow called Mum's the Word, a rewrite of Blind Date for modern society in which the young children of single mothers select a man for her to take out on a date.

In America, John McEnroe is presiding over The Chair, which sounds like The Weakest Link remodelled by a South American police force. Contestants in this quiz are wired to monitors which record their pulse rate. In a rule which is supposed to reward the cool, they lose points if they develop palpitations under McEnroe's questioning.

However the press releases may present them, both these series have terrifying premises. In the British show, children who have experienced divorce or other family fragmentation are encouraged to live out the dream or fear of a new father figure in front of millions of viewers. Promises of responsibility have been made by the producers but any programme controller offered this synopsis would surely realise that the series could only become compelling viewing if the children started plotting against certain contestants.

As for The Chair, the rules of that game ask viewers to laugh at signs of cardiac distress, with the ultimate possibility that the studio audience will discover they have just given a round of applause to a heart attack. Medical screening and disclaimer forms will presumably be employed but they cannot avoid the fact that, when rats and mice are treated to such primitive stress tests, there are pickets outside the laboratory gates.

Neither of these series, though, should be a surprise to viewers of Channel 4's current fourth instalment series of Big Brother. The previous three series (and especially the celebrity edition) were responsibly edited and psychologically revealing. Most of the contestants could look after themselves and, if they couldn't, the producers did. But, this time, vulnerable participants have been subjected to trivial humiliations in exchange for their desperation for fame. The character of Jade has suffered the sort of brutal newspaper coverage usually reserved for serial killers and women who marry into the royal family, her face compared to a pig's and her brain to an amoeba's.

The idea of Big Brother was to film real people and plot and edit their activities like a drama: the above reference to Jade as a 'character' was deliberate. But what's now happening is that newspapers are writing about the participants as if they were fictional characters. The problem is that J R Ewing and Janine in EastEnders aren't going to weep when they read what's been written about them or risk attacks in the street.

Or – and this is crucial – sue the television companies. While participants in TV shows are routinely asked to sign forms absolving the networks of responsibility, the 'hotel room corpse' case in America signals that the next big wave of litigation is likely to involve people exploited by TV shows. On the wall of every producer of 'reality' TV should hang the legend: 'These people are human.'

In the 1970s, those speculating about the ultimate in bad-taste television – either in panel discussions or science-fiction stories – would usually suggest the live transmission of sex, murder, suicide or execution. Though none of these activities has ever been transmitted as it happens, all have now been broadcast within the context of documentaries. The Internet increases the chances of such deaths going out live.

The makers of Mum's the Word apparently hope that the children of their single mothers will make cute or smart remarks. Here's something sassy for one of them to say: no adult who agreed to be a contestant in that show should be allowed near children at all.

Before you read

Create a spider diagram to pick out the different reality TV shows mentioned in the article. Say what happens in each show.

Reading for meaning

1 What is the significance of the title of the article?

2 a) How has the purpose and content of television changed over the past thirty years according to the author of the article?

   b) How are reality TV shows changing?

3 What criticisms does the article make of reality TV shows?

4 a) What attitude does the author of the article have towards current reality TV shows?

   b) Find words or phrases or imagery that indicate a **biased** or negative attitude.

   c) Find any examples of **irony**.

5 Would you say this article comes from a tabloid or a broadsheet? Justify your answer in terms of:

   • structure and organisation
   • language
   • style
   • tone.

Sentences and paragraphs

1 Summarise the main point of each paragraph in the article.

2 For each paragraph, identify:

   • a key sentence or topic sentence that indicates the main idea
   • the parts that develop the main idea or give examples to support the main idea
   • a point that links to previous or later paragraphs.

Drama

1 As a class, brainstorm the characteristics that would make a successful contestant in Big Brother.

2 In groups of four, prepare an audition for the next series of the programme. One of you will be the applicant. All of you will prepare the material. Your audition should take the form of a two-minute video and should:

- emphasise the good aspects of the applicant's personality
- explain what the applicant could offer the show
- be persuasive
- be bubbly and energetic.

3 Present your audition to the rest of the class.

4 As a class, compare and analyse the performances and select two people who would make the best contestants on Big Brother.

Speaking and listening

S&L 9

In pairs, identify arguments for and against reality TV shows.

- One of you should argue the positive aspects of reality TV.
- One of you should argue the negative aspects of reality TV.
- Listen to each other's point of view and be prepared to disagree and contradict.

Writing to analyse, review and comment

Write an essay about the positive and negative aspects of reality TV, using material from the *Speaking and listening* task, evidence from the article and your own experience.

- Provide a clear introduction to the issue.
- Develop your argument.
- Draw your argument together with a well-considered conclusion.
- Use standard English and check the accuracy of your spelling, punctuation and grammar.

Writing to inform, explain and describe

Write a formal report to the Television Standards Committee warning of the dangers of reality TV shows and the way the contestants are treated.

Use appropriate sub-headings for your report. Open with a clear introduction and end with a suitable conclusion.

You could include in your report:

- the way the contestants are treated
- the development of reality TV shows
- the future of this type of TV programme.

A written **report** should:

- make it clear who the report is written to
- use a good title that sums up what the report is about
- contain a clear introduction to the issue
- use sub-headings to separate the main points
- end with a conclusion that features a solution to the problem the report is tackling.

Use standard English and formal vocabulary throughout when you are writing a report. You might decide to use the **passive voice** to increase the sense of objectivity.

Before you write, plan your ideas and think about how you are going to construct and link your paragraphs.

Survivor

This is an extract from an interview with Charlotte Hobrough, the winner of the first series of 'Survivor', a reality TV game show. She was named 'Ultimate Survivor' and won one million pounds after living on the remote island of Pulau Tiga and beating off competition from all the other contestants. The interview was conducted after the series had been broadcast and Charlotte had returned from the island.

Research

1 Find out as much as you can about the game show format for 'Survivor'.

2 What do you think would be hard or enjoyable about being a contestant on 'Survivor'?

3 What qualities would make a good contestant in this show?

As you read

Consider how Charlotte describes her experiences on the island. Was her experience generally positive or negative?

dor

Survivor

SURVIVOR

When we spoke last it was before the programme aired. What has it been like over the past couple of months, not only waiting to see if you won the million, but also to watch yourself on TV and all the tabloid press that went with it?

At first I thought surviving after Survivor was going to be harder than surviving on the island. But things have got a lot better. At the start there were some horrendous reports stemming from people like JJ and they were so nasty. I find that quite incredible because on the island JJ and I got on quite well, I think. She just showed extreme bitterness which let her down a bit. Even though Zoë and myself all had our moments of screaming and arguing with each other, when they got back home with the people they love, they came on the Survivor Unseen show and showed their true personalities, which were not like some of the nasty things they said on the island. Hopefully, I have done the same. I haven't been all roses while on the island but I have come back and people have, hopefully, seen the real me.

What do you say now to those people who were quick to pass judgement on you?

I would say, 'It's amazing how far you get being fluffy and useless.'

Who was the person that you were least looking forward to being reunited with this evening?

JJ definitely. It has to be. I thought she was particularly nasty and vindictive. She has shown aggressive verbal behaviour towards me and some of the things she has been saying are beyond belief. She lives near me and she has been saying some awful things. I kept thinking, 'It's only a game.' If I had not won tonight I would still have seen it as a game. Mark, my husband, and I had decided it was up to fate. JJ got voted out and she had it coming and she was so intent on her own opinions that she had no idea what anyone else was thinking. Her listening skills were terrible and certainly need to improve if she ever wants to go in for a show like this again.

Were you surprised by the 7–0 vote in your favour?

Yes. Mark had to tell me because by the fourth vote I had won and I did not realise what was going on from then on, because I was so shocked. Mick's vote was the biggest surprise. He and Jackie really, really got on well but what it showed me was that people did look at the decision objectively. It is not about whom you really liked and whom you got on with the best, or about tribal loyalties. They looked at us as individuals and I am really pleased they did that.

What do you think was the secret of your success?

Determination, I would say. I was always determined to get to the end and win. I had some bad days, as everyone saw. But I pulled myself out of that and showed determination. The turning point was seeing that video from home, which gave me a lot of strength. On that island, you did not have anyone else. Seeing Mark and my Mum pitched me straight back into reality and I was able to snap myself out of that depression. I was back in the game then, I was chatting to Jackie and to Richard. It wasn't just surface chat, we really got on well and I realised I was there for a purpose, they didn't just feel sorry for me.

Is there anything you would like to say to Jackie?

Jackie, I think you are fantastic. You deserve it just as much as me. We are both winners because we both made the final. You are a truly great person and I really, really hope that we will be friends for a very long time.

On the show that was filmed before you went on the island, Meet the Survivors, you said that if you won then you would spend the money on flash cars and diamonds. At the last Tribal Council, however, you mentioned that you would pay off your mortgage and help your family out. Was it the case that you played down your true intentions with the money so as not to damage your chances with the jury?

No, not really. That's how I intend to spend the money and if there's enough left to pay for cars and diamonds then we will see. I told Mark when I got back that I got through to the final two. He started talking about sensible things and how great it would be not to have these massive lumps of money coming out of your wages every month to go on the house. If we pay off the mortgage, that will give us more money in the long run. I do think sensibly about it. A million pounds is an awful lot of money. It's a fantastic amount of money and just enough to ensure Mark and I have a fantastic life and make my family as happy as I possibly can.

How has the experience on the island changed you?

I feel I have become a stronger person, stronger being on my own and more confident and more adaptable. I feel I am able to appreciate things more. It is amazing how lovely it is to clean your teeth every morning. Just the smallest little things like that I really missed. The main thing is being able to be on my own. That is something I have never been good at in my life. I have three sisters and one brother and we have always been a bit of a tribe. I'm married now as well so I am always with people and I found being on my own very difficult. At the merger[1], I was very isolated and I had to learn to live with that. I learnt to sit, think and enjoy my own company.

Given all the publicity and all the vitriol directed at you from some quarters, was it all worth a million pounds?

For a million pounds, yes it was. There have been some very difficult times and some things have been totally blown out of all proportion but the money will make me, my husband and my family very happy so, yes, that makes it all worthwhile.

---

1 The two 'tribes' were merged once enough contestants had been eliminated.

Reading for meaning

1 What does the interviewer's first question tell you about the way in which 'Survivor' was set up, filmed, broadcast and judged?

2 a) What is revealed about Charlotte's character in the interview? *Hint: Think about her tone and how she speaks as well as what she says.*

   b) What is revealed about her tactics for winning?

3 How does Charlotte feel about her fellow contestants?

4 What evidence can you find in the interview of how 'Survivor' was reported in the press and in the media?

5 a) Do you think that being in 'Survivor' has been a positive or a negative experience for Charlotte?

   b) How might being on 'Survivor' affect the contestants negatively?

Sentences, paragraphs and cohesion

1 How is the interview extract structured? Divide it into subsections with headings.

2 How many open and how many closed questions does the interviewer ask?

3 The interviewer gives no responses to what Charlotte says, but sticks to pre-prepared questions. How might you respond and what additional follow-up questions would you ask?

4 a) The text is a written version of a spoken interview. To what extent does it show features of spoken English? *Hint: pauses, hesitations, incomplete sentences, use of contracted forms (I'm not I am)*

   b) Why do you think these changes to the spoken version have been made?

Writing to imagine, explore and entertain

Imagine you have been stranded on a remote tropical island. Write a first-person account of a day in your journal. You should include:

- how you spend your day
- how you hunt for food
- what you think of the other people who are with you
- how you plan to get off the island
- how you feel.

Speaking and listening

As a group, discuss what you think it would be like to be a contestant on 'Survivor'. How would this experience compare to being a contestant on 'Big Brother'?

Writing to compare

Write an extended essay to compare 'Survivor' and 'Big Brother'. In what ways is 'Survivor' similar to 'Big Brother' and in what ways is it different?

- Look back at the work you have done on the two programmes and draw up a table like the one on below to organise your thoughts.

	Survivor	Big Brother
Format		
Prize money		
Showing times and frequency		
Broadcast live? **Extent to which it is edited**		
Level of pressure on contestants **Dangers**		
Support given to contestants		
Press coverage		
Accompanying marketing		

- In your conclusion state which show you think is better and why.
- Use standard English and check the accuracy of your spelling, punctuation and grammar.

GCSE Coursework question

In this task you will start to develop those skills needed to fulfil the written coursework requirements of GCSE. Study of media is part of all GCSE specification criteria either as a question within the examination or, as in this task, a coursework essay. The media coursework unit makes up 5% of the total marks awarded for your GCSE.

Media Coursework: Writing to analyse, review and comment

Analyse the genre of Reality TV by comparing at least two examples from this genre.

There is no prescribed length for this piece of coursework. It will be assessed on the effectiveness of your writing and how well you have achieved your task. You should avoid writing something excessively long, though.

In your essay, you should consider the following:

- A definition of Reality TV

- An outline explanation of the format and rules of two Reality TV shows

- The purpose of Reality TV shows

- How editing and camera work is used to create the storyline

- How the 'characters' are presented to us

- The success of Reality TV

- Overall, what you think of Reality TV.

5.2 The Internet

In this section you are going to be looking at and comparing two websites for TV channels. You will look at the interactivity, features, content and how each website aims to attract and influence its target audience.

Speaking and listening

1 In a group, discuss how you use the Internet. How often do you use it? When? What sites do you use?

2 In your group, prepare a list of your top five recommended sites. Say:
   • what sort of site each one is
   • what its features are
   • why you like it.

Trouble TV Online

> Trouble TV is a commercial television channel that runs a Trouble TV website.

Reading for meaning

1 a) Look at the homepage of the Trouble TV website on page 224. From this homepage, identify as closely as you can the target audience of this website. *Hint: Think about age, gender, interest, spending power.*

  b) Comment on how the following features help us to gain a picture of the audience:

  • graphics, colours and pictures
  • list of contents on the navigation bar and special features
  • targeting of the adverts on the site
  • tone and style of the language used.

2 Unlike printed forms of media, the content of websites is never fixed and is frequently updated. Identify features on the homepage on page 224 that would change and estimate how often you think they would change.

3 How do you think the 'temporary' nature of a website affects the content and style of this site?

4 Why do you think Trouble TV runs a website? *Hint: Think about whether it is to make a profit from the site or to encourage viewing.*

5 Look at the site map of the Trouble TV website on page 225. How many screens would you have to go through to get to:

a) the Daniel Bedingfield 'Gotta Get Thru This' review

b) a factsheet on bullying?

6 How does navigating a website make it a different experience from that of, for example, reading through a magazine?

Live Home Page
Apple Computer
Apple Support
Apple Store
Microsoft MacTopia
MSN
Office for Macintosh
TROUBLE T
ALL THE INTERNET YOU WANT ANYTIME YOU WANT IT
freeserve anytime
THE LIST
TROUBLE TV
CHAT ZONE
THE CLINIC
GAMES
CARTOONS
TROUBLE MUSIC
MAKE UR OWN SITE
SHOPPING MALL
RINGTONES & LOGOS
FLASH BOYFRIEND
FLASH BAND
how to get TV
celebrity eXtra
The latest news on the hottest celebs...
NOW: In the House, 15:30
NEXT: The Fresh Prince of Bel Air, 16:00
On Trouble.co.uk
NEW BAND NEED MANAGER
WHO DA MAN
DAILY VOTE
Do you believe everything you read in the papers?
Yes No VOTE
Star Style Fashion
ASOS.com
Dress like Jen or Brad! ASOS has what you want.
Ronan Goodies
Watch Ronan live from your bedroom!
Celebrity Corner
Catch up with the Appleton sisters.
CHAT
Chat on TV
Find out how to chat when your brother is hogging ur PC!
New Music Now!
What's new from Daniel Bedingfield? Find out now!
D-side!
Introducing D-Side. All LUSH and 100% Irish. Taste 'em.
SCORPION KING
The Scorpion King Your chance to win loadsa goodies right here, right now!
TERMS + CONDITIONS
ADVERTISE
CONTACT US
© Flextech Television 2001-2002
Internet zone

Site map for Trouble TV

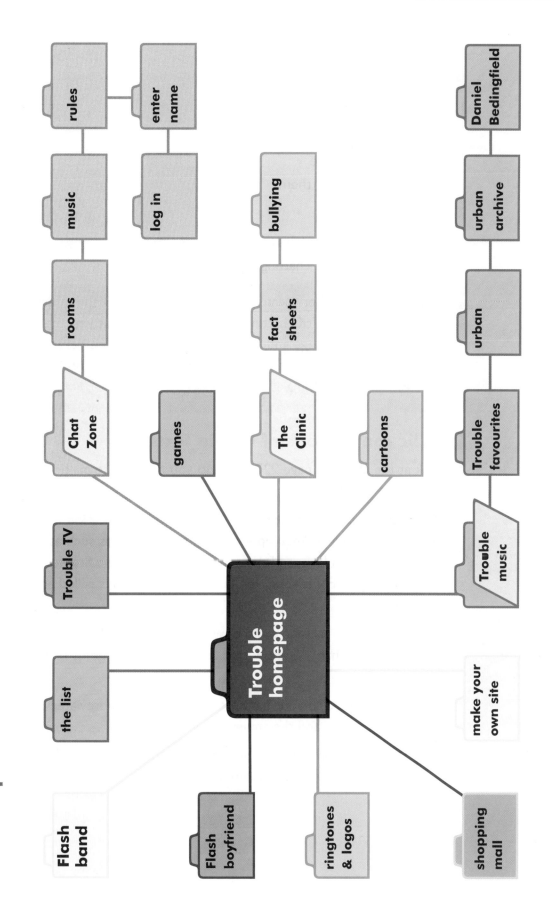

Cyber Chat

Before you read

1   As a class, find out:

- how many of you have used chatrooms
- which ones you use
- how often you use them.

2   Discuss:

- What is good about 'chatting' on the Internet?
- What is bad about 'chatting' on the Internet?

Chat rooms are another means of communication using the Internet. One of the drawbacks of chatting via the Internet is that you are unaware of body language and non-verbal signals from the person you are communicating with. The chart opposite shows 'emoticons' or 'smileys' used to summarise emotion.

Stylistic conventions of media texts

1   Look at the chart on page 227. Why do you think these particular symbols have been used?

2   One of the features of chat rooms is speed. Communication is fast and sometimes difficult to keep up with. Abbreviated words such as 'u' for 'you' are used, and longer phrases are shortened to the first letters of each word e.g. TTFN is short for Ta Ta For Now. This is called an **acronym**.

a) Working with a partner, write down as many examples of abbreviations that you know that are used in chat rooms or in 'txt' messaging.

b) Write a message to your partner using both the abbreviated 'txt' messaging words and the smileys to indicate mood.

c) Try writing this on the computer. What happens to some of the emoticons when you type them in?

Emoticon	Emotion
:-)	happy
:-(	sad
:-<	very sad or upset
:-O	shocked or amazed
:-D	laughing
;-)	winking
:-|	bored or uninterested
8-|	what next!
8-O	extremely shocked
:-]	smirk, happy sarcasm
:-[	grimace, sad sarcasm
:-}	grinning
:-\	undecided
:-#	sealed lips
:-&	tongue-tied
:-I	hmmm

Writing to imagine, explore and entertain

Using the conventions of chat, write an imaginary conversation between four people communicating via either:

- a music chat room
- a sport chat room
- a film chat room
- a hobby chat room.

You should give yourself a nickname and use the same layout as you would find in a chat room.

Daniel Bedingfield 'Gotta Get Thru This'

Before you read

1 Only the most up-to-date reviews are kept on the Trouble TV website. Why?

2 Think about the process of clicking through or surfing sites. How does your reading style differ from reading a book or a magazine? *Hint: Do you skim read? How long will you spend looking at a piece? Will you read everything?*

3 How does your approach to reading material on a web page affect the way in which webtext has been written? *Hint: Think about length, impact, style.*

Reading for meaning

1 What facts does the review on page 229 give about the track and the artist?

2 How would you describe the tone of this review and the attitude of this review to the track?

3 a) List the references to other music or artists mentioned in the review.

   b) What is the effect of making these references? Do you recognise them all?

   c) How does the use of reference define the target audience?

4 What rhetorical devices can you identify in this review?

5 Identify examples of irony and humour.

Vocabulary and sentences

**Sn 3
Sn 7**

1 a) Find examples of subject-specialist vocabulary used in the review to talk about music.

   b) Find examples of non-standard English in this writing.

2 Why does the writer choose to use this sort of language?

Writing to analyse, review and comment

1 Imitate the style of the Daniel Bedingfield review and write a review of a track you know for the Trouble TV website.

2 Now write a parallel review of the same track for a broadsheet newspaper.

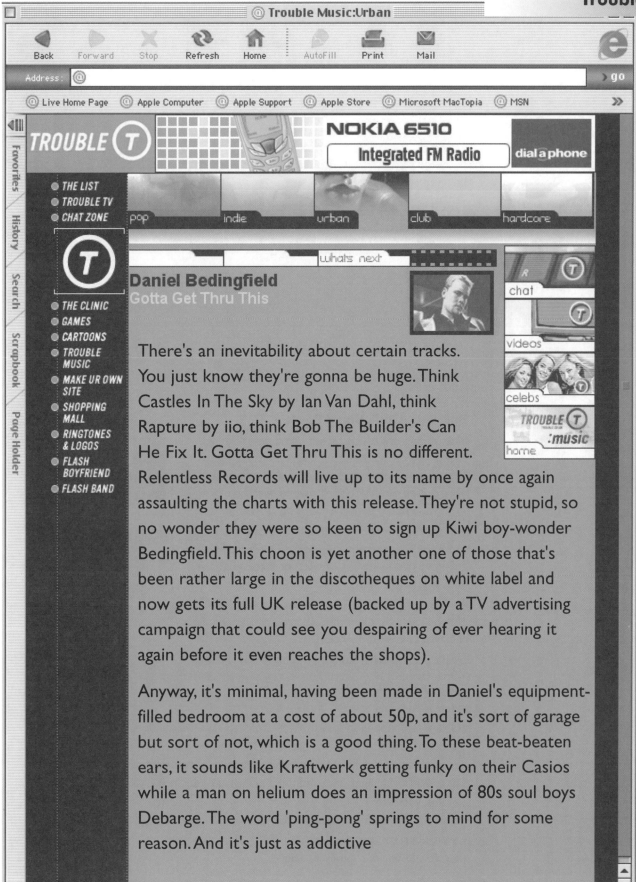

@ Trouble Music:Urban

Back Forward Stop Refresh Home AutoFill Print Mail

Address: @

> go

@ Live Home Page   @ Apple Computer   @ Apple Support   @ Apple Store   @ Microsoft MacTopia   @ MSN   »

TROUBLE (T)

NOKIA 6510
Integrated FM Radio
dial a phone

- THE LIST
- TROUBLE TV
- CHAT ZONE

pop   indie   urban   club   hardcore

whats next

Daniel Bedingfield
Gotta Get Thru This

- THE CLINIC
- GAMES
- CARTOONS
- TROUBLE MUSIC
- MAKE UR OWN SITE
- SHOPPING MALL
- RINGTONES & LOGOS
- FLASH BOYFRIEND
- FLASH BAND

chat

videos

celebs

TROUBLE (T) :music

home

There's an inevitability about certain tracks. You just know they're gonna be huge. Think Castles In The Sky by Ian Van Dahl, think Rapture by iio, think Bob The Builder's Can He Fix It. Gotta Get Thru This is no different. Relentless Records will live up to its name by once again assaulting the charts with this release. They're not stupid, so no wonder they were so keen to sign up Kiwi boy-wonder Bedingfield. This choon is yet another one of those that's been rather large in the discotheques on white label and now gets its full UK release (backed up by a TV advertising campaign that could see you despairing of ever hearing it again before it even reaches the shops).

Anyway, it's minimal, having been made in Daniel's equipment-filled bedroom at a cost of about 50p, and it's sort of garage but sort of not, which is a good thing. To these beat-beaten ears, it sounds like Kraftwerk getting funky on their Casios while a man on helium does an impression of 80s soul boys Debarge. The word 'ping-pong' springs to mind for some reason. And it's just as addictive

Internet zone

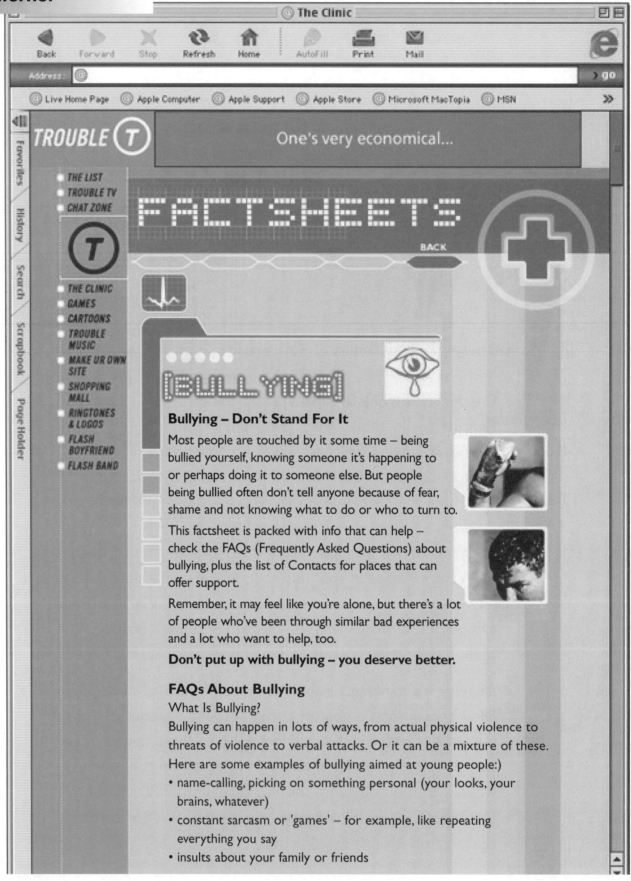

@ The Clinic

Back · Forward · Stop · Refresh · Home · AutoFill · Print · Mail

Address: @

Live Home Page · Apple Computer · Apple Support · Apple Store · Microsoft MacTopia · MSN

TROUBLE (T)

One's very economical...

- THE LIST
- TROUBLE TV
- CHAT ZONE

(T)

- THE CLINIC
- GAMES
- CARTOONS
- TROUBLE MUSIC
- MAKE UR OWN SITE
- SHOPPING MALL
- RINGTONES & LOGOS
- FLASH BOYFRIEND
- FLASH BAND

FACTSHEETS

BACK

[BULLYING]

Bullying – Don't Stand For It

Most people are touched by it some time – being bullied yourself, knowing someone it's happening to or perhaps doing it to someone else. But people being bullied often don't tell anyone because of fear, shame and not knowing what to do or who to turn to.

This factsheet is packed with info that can help – check the FAQs (Frequently Asked Questions) about bullying, plus the list of Contacts for places that can offer support.

Remember, it may feel like you're alone, but there's a lot of people who've been through similar bad experiences and a lot who want to help, too.

Don't put up with bullying – you deserve better.

FAQs About Bullying

What Is Bullying?

Bullying can happen in lots of ways, from actual physical violence to threats of violence to verbal attacks. Or it can be a mixture of these. Here are some examples of bullying aimed at young people:)

- name-calling, picking on something personal (your looks, your brains, whatever)
- constant sarcasm or 'games' – for example, like repeating everything you say
- insults about your family or friends

- grabbing your possessions – bag, Walkman etc. – and throwing them round, looking through them, damaging them, mocking them
- blackmail (saying if you don't do certain things, like give them your money, they'll do something bad to you)
- spreading rumours about you
- ignoring you or leaving you out on purpose
- pushing, shoving or grabbing your body or clothes
- hitting, punching, pulling your hair, kicking you etc.
- threatening you – threatening to physically attack or do other things to you
- insulting or attacking you because of your colour, race or religion
- insulting or attacking you because you're gay or bisexual

There are other variations, but they all use power and fear to make the person being bullied feel bad and give in.

Isn't It Just Part Of Growing Up?

Everyone gets ratty sometimes and snaps at people, even at their friends, and that's a normal part of being a human. But bullying is different from that. It's picking on someone, doing it on purpose, wanting to hurt the person, trying to use power and intimidation to make them feel bad. It's picking on someone who can't easily defend themselves. At times, somebody (perhaps an adult) may tell you it's just part of growing up and that it will make you a stronger person, but actual bullying is not all right and nobody deserves to be treated like this.

Only Weak People Get Picked On...

No - it's the bully who's acting weak, not the person they're bullying. Loads of different people become victims of bullying sometime in their lives. A massive variety, including people who go on to be mega-famous. Some of these are mentioned on the web sites listed below. Often, one bully targets more than one person to intimidate, so it might not just be you.

Remember, the bully chooses victims, not the other way round.

Reading for meaning

1   The Trouble TV website includes factsheets on: illegal drugs, sex and sexuality, bullying and eating disorders. What does this tell you about the site's target audience and its relationship with its audience?

2   Comment on the organisation and layout of the text in the factsheet extract and say how it might read as a webtext.

3   a) What features of this text are informal and speech-like? Find examples.

   b) How does the style of writing affect the 'tone of voice' that the piece has?

CiTV Online

You are now going to look at CiTV Online; the website run by children's ITV. While you are working through this section, you should refer to the live version of CiTV Online on the Internet.

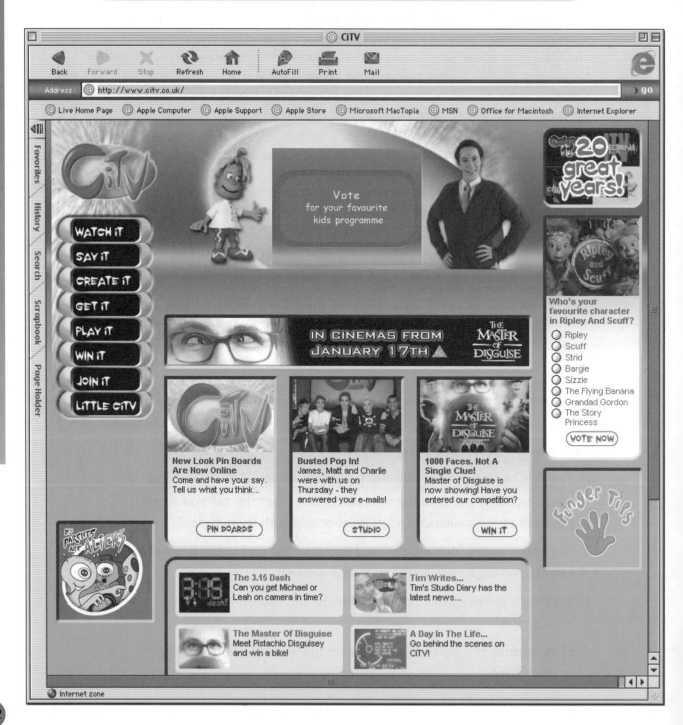

As you read

Look at the website online. Consider how this website differs from the one for Trouble TV. You could consider:

- the content of each of the sites
- how you move around the sites
- the layout of the text and the images on each of the sites
- the images chosen for each site and what they add
- the style of each site
- the intended audience for each site.

Reading for meaning

1 a) What age group is this website aimed at? How does this differ from the age group Trouble TV's website aims at? *Hint: Look at the graphics and design, content and features and at the language used.*

   b) How else would the target audience for CiTV Online be different from that of Trouble TV's?

2 From which country do the majority of the television programmes come? How does this differ from Trouble TV?

3 List the different ways in which viewers can 'be part of CiTV'. Why do you think ITV would want to create a web 'community'?

4 How does the website encourage surfers to keep returning to it?

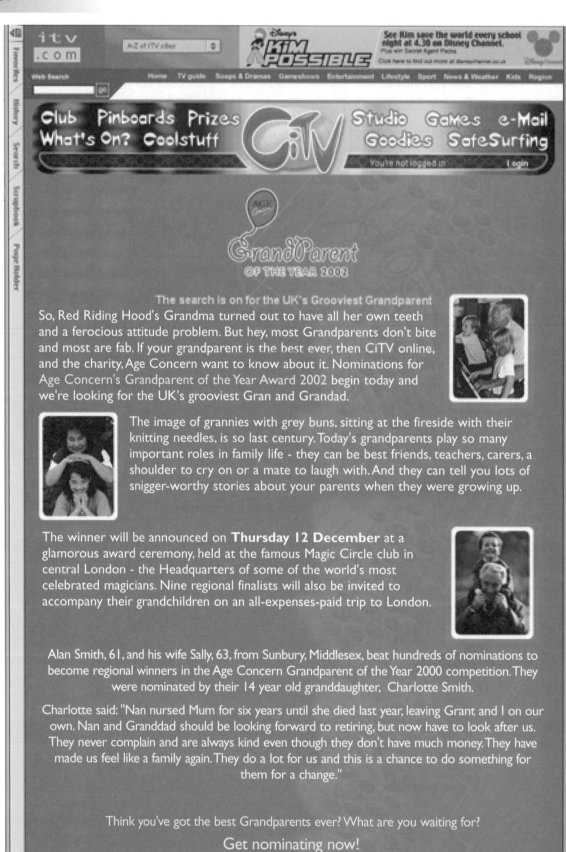

Reading for meaning

Look at the 'Grandparent of the Year' web page on page 234.

1   What features of this web page are typical of material on the web?
Hint: Look at design, layout, organisation, length and style.

2   a) What is the purpose of using stereotypical views of grandparents?

b) What is the intended impact of referring to Little Red Riding Hood?

c) How does the web page try to promote a positive attitude towards grandparents?

3   a) What does the link with the charity Age Concern tell you about the values promoted by the website?

b) Compare these values with the values promoted by the Trouble TV website.

4   What does this page tell you about the intended audience?

Wr 9

Vocabulary and sentences

The language on the 'Grandparent of the Year' web page creates a friendly and enthusiastic tone.

a) Pick out words and phrases that are informal and non-standard.

b) Find examples of more speech-like patterns of sentence structure.

Writing to inform, explain and describe

Write a detailed explanation of how chat rooms operate and the potential benefits and dangers of using them.

Imagine that the person reading your explanation has a limited understanding of the Internet, and has never used a chatroom before.

Consider the following points for your explanation:

* how chat rooms work
* who can talk in a chat room
* the topics that can be discussed
* the benefits of using chat rooms
* the potential dangers of using chat rooms
* how to use chat rooms safely.

GCSE Coursework question

In this task you will start to develop those skills needed to fulfil the written coursework requirements of GCSE. Study of media is part of all GCSE Specification criteria either as a question within the examination or, as in this task, a coursework essay. The media coursework unit makes up 5% of the total marks awarded for your GCSE.

Media Coursework: Writing to analyse, review and comment

Compare and contrast the websites CiTV online and Trouble TV online

There is no prescribed length for this piece of coursework. It will be assessed on the effectiveness of your writing and how well you have achieved your task. You should avoid writing something excessively long, though.

In your essay, you should consider the following:

- Content – what variety of articles/features is there?

- Purpose – what is the purpose of the websites?

- Use of images – are there photos, moving images, pictures, cartoons? In what ways do the images enhance the site?

- Graphics – think about the use of lettering, colour, variety of font, variety of size.

- Writing – what writing style is used? How is the writing organised?

- Layout – use of bullet points, text boxes, balance of pictures to text?

- Navigation – how do you move around the site? How clear is movement around the site?

- Audience – what gender, age, social background, language use? How well does the website suit its target audience?

- Overall – what is your response to the sites?

The Shakespeare paper

▶ You will have 1 hour and 15 minutes to complete the Shakespeare paper.

▶ The paper is made up of two parts: SECTION A The Short Writing Task and SECTION B The Shakespeare Reading Task.

SECTION A The Short Writing Task

▶ You should spend **30 minutes** on the Short Writing Task; **5 minutes** of this time should be spent planning.

▶ The task will ask you to write for **one** of the following purposes:

- to imagine, explore, entertain
- to persuade, argue, advise
- to inform, explain, describe
- to analyse, review, comment.

You will **not** be marked on your knowledge of the Shakespeare play in the Short Writing Task. You will be marked on your ability to write **appropriately** and **accurately** for the **audience** and **purpose** given in the task. You will be marked for:

▶ **sentence structure, punctuation** and **text organisation** (8 marks) Sentence structures need to be varied and suited to the purpose and audience of the task. You will also need to use a variety of punctuation accurately to make meaning clear and create effects.

▶ **composition and effect** (8 marks) This is about the content and the way you express yourself. Your writing needs to be appropriate to the purpose and audience of the task. You will need to think about the style and tone of your writing.

▶ **spelling** (4 marks) Spelling needs to be accurate. That doesn't mean you should only use simple words, though! You won't get top marks if you do.

Don't try to write too much. This is a *short* writing task and quality is much more important than quantity.

▶ There are a maximum of **20 marks** available for the Short Writing Task.

SECTION A The Short Writing task

Writing to imagine, explore, entertain

Example

In the play, Macbeth receives bad news: his wife is ill and he is about to fight against an army.

You write soap opera-scripts for a TV company. You have received the following:

> MEMO
>
> **Urgent for the next episode.**
>
> Viewers think life has become too happy for our community! We need to introduce some bad news! This could be an illness in the family, difficulties with friends or trouble at work.
>
> You decide, but make it tense and really put the feelings of the character across.
>
> It only needs to be a few minutes long – we can tell more of the story in future episodes.

Write the script of this part of the episode, where the character receives the bad news. (20 marks)

Examiner's comments

*The main task is given in **bold** print and is introduced by some information to help you to respond. In this example, you are told the **audience** for your writing (viewers of a TV programme), the **purpose** of the writing (to create tension), the **type** of writing (script), and are given some ideas about **content** (the nature of the bad news).*

Planning

Before you start you should spend a few minutes noting down some key points and deciding how you will express and organise them.

Content

You are given a choice of 'bad news' for your character(s) to receive. Remember that you don't have to reveal everything.

It is a script for a TV programme, so do include sound effects, setting information and acting instructions.

Organisation and style

This is a **script.** You will need to use the features of this text type:

- layout: make it clear which words are spoken and which is information for the actors

- stage directions can be in note form if they are short

- dialogue: the characters might not all speak in the same way. The person bringing the bad news might be more formal than the character receiving it. Give them their own 'voice' through your choice of vocabulary and sentence structures.

Here is part of a script written by a student in response to this task.

SETTING: LINDA'S HOUSE. THE TV IS ON BUT SHE ISN'T REALLY WATCHING. HER SON, MIKE, IS OUT. HE SHOULD HAVE BEEN BACK BY NOW.

SFX: CRUNCH OF SHOES ON THE GRAVEL PATH

LINDA ATTENTIVELY WAITS TO HEAR THE KEY IN THE DOOR BUT INSTEAD THERE IS A FIRM KNOCK. FRUSTRATED THAT THIS ISN'T MIKE HOME, LINDA OPENS THE DOOR. SHE IS GREETED BY A POLICE OFFICER, HIS COLLEAGUE STANDING SLIGHTLY BEHIND HIM, LOOKING AT THE HOUSE AND GARDEN AS HE WAITS.

OFFICER 1: I'm PC Walker. And this is PC Fletcher. Is Mike Peterson in, please?

LINDA: [NERVOUSLY] Er, no officer. He's late. I've been expecting him this last hour or more. He's usually very punctual, a good lad, you know. Don't know what's keeping him today, though. His dinner has gone cold, too. That's not like him, missing a meal ...

OFFICER 2: [INTERRUPTING] Do you have any idea where he might be, madam?

LINDA: Er, no. He didn't say. That's not like him, either, come to think of it. He does normally tell me where he's going. We get on well like that. Why? What's the problem? He isn't in trouble is he? I mean ...

OFFICER 1: [INTERRUPTING] Well, let's just say we need to talk to him, to eliminate him from our enquiries. Now, madam, will you ask him to call this number when he returns?

LINDA TAKES THE NUMBER, LOOKING ANXIOUS.

Examiner's comments

This is the beginning of the dialogue. The scene (mum waiting for son to come home) has already been set. Here, the differences between the characters are made clear. Linda is rambling in her speech, which is informal (while the officers' speech is formal ('eliminate him from our enquiries') and clipped ('Is Mike Peterson in, please?'). The stage directions also support this. Linda is 'nervous' while the officers have to interrupt. The script is set out so the dialogue and the stage directions are easily distinguished.

Practice

Now write your own response to this task.

Writing to inform, explain and describe

Example

In *Macbeth*, Duncan is the Macbeths' special guest.

Your school has invited a special guest to give a talk in assembly. You have been chosen to give the welcome speech. After speaking to your teacher, you have made the following notes about what to say:

> Welcome speech
> • Introduce guest – give info about guest
> • Thank them for attending – say purpose of visit
> • Give info about what will happen during assembly/duration of visit
> • Be formal and polite (bit of humour is OK)
> • Must be clear and logical for listeners to follow

Write the speech you will give. Your teacher wants to check it before the event! (20 marks)

Examiner's comments

*The main task is given in **bold** print and is introduced by some information that will help you to respond. In this example, you are told the **audience** for your writing (special guest and students in assembly), the **purpose** of the writing (to introduce the guest), the **type** of writing (speech), and are given some ideas about the **content** (information about the guest).*

Planning

Before you start you should spend a few minutes noting down some key points and deciding how you will express and organise them. The notes provided in the example above give you one way of structuring the information. You are also given information on the style and tone of the speech.

Content

You will need to give brief information about the special guest, mention a few achievements, give information about the reason for the visit and what will happen during the visit. Most of all, you need to prepare the audience for the guest's talk.

Organisation and style

This is a **speech**. You will need to use the features of this text type:

- the style and tone needed is polite and formal (you want to make a good impression)
- it needs to be positive and 'welcoming'
- listeners can't reread the information so it is particularly important that it is clear and easy to follow
- you will sometimes address the guest directly (using '*you*') or indirectly (using their name/'*he*' or '*she*'). Other parts of the speech will address the students directly (using '*you*' – or '*we*', as you are also one of the students).

Here is part of a speech written by a student in response to this task.

Today, it is my great pleasure to welcome David Beckham to speak at our assembly. As I'm sure you all know, David is a hugely talented footballer and I'm sure is an enormous inspiration to many of our players at school. Not only does he play for one of the best teams in the premiership, Manchester United, but he has also captained England on many memorable occasions. He is also a proud father and, despite his celebrity status, he tries to find time to spend with his family.

Examiner's comments

The special guest is introduced immediately, as is the purpose of the visit (to speak at the assembly). The opening is formal ('it is my great pleasure') and positive in tone. The first person is used to give a personal feel to it. Many positive phrases are used to describe the guest ('inspiration', 'talented') – with adjectives ('enormous', 'best', 'memorable') and adverbs ('hugely') to increase the compliments. His achievements are emphasised by the phrase 'not only ... but ...'. Different aspects of his life are briefly considered so that he could appeal to people in the audience with different interests. The sentences are mostly complex, so that lots of information is communicated concisely.

What might this student write about next? How might the speech go on?

Practice

Now write your own response to this task.

Writing to persuade, argue, advise

Example

In *Macbeth*, Macbeth argues why he should not kill Duncan.

Your headteacher placed the following notice on the year group notice board. It gives some of the reasons why the request by students for an end of year disco has been rejected.

End-of-year disco

A disco has been proposed by students again. It is the view of the teachers that it should not be allowed to go ahead.

- In the past, there has been trouble at this event and the end-of-year discos were banned for many years.
- There is not time for the all the litter to be cleared up before the PE lessons in the hall the following day.
- Teachers have to give up their evening to supervise and they are busy finishing off reports at this time.

Prepare the written argument you will present at the next school council meeting to persuade the headteacher to reverse the decision. (20 marks)

Examiner's comments

*The main task is given in **bold** print and is introduced by some information that will help you to respond. In this example, you are told the **audience** for your writing (school council), the **purpose** of the writing (to argue a point of view), the **type** of writing (persuasive), and are given some ideas about the **content** (points to argue against).*

Content

You need to give counter-arguments for the three main points made by the headteacher. You might want to introduce briefly some other opinions. You could give evidence to support your case and offer solutions to the problems the headteacher has raised. Remember that the headteacher will be present at the council meeting, so you must be sympathetic to his or her concerns!

Organisation and style

This is **persuasive** writing. You should use the features of this text type:

• adopt a formal tone

• use first person (singular or plural) as personal views are given

• active voice (or passive voice to avoid naming those doing the actions)

• connectives to show logic ('therefore', 'in fact')

• use persuasive devices (rhetorical questions; lists of three; adjectives and adverbs to affect the reader emotionally).

Here is the beginning of the written argument prepared by a student in response to this task.

The students in Y9 are, understandably, disappointed to learn that their request for a disco has been rejected. While the concerns are viewed sympathetically, as a representative of the year group I am seeking to persuade the teachers to change their minds. I also have some practical solutions to offer that I hope will support our cause.

Examiner's comments

The main point is immediately introduced (disco request rejected). The tone is formal. This is achieved through the complex sentence structures ('while the concerns are viewed sympathetically, as a representative ..., I am ...') and formal phrasing ('seeking to persuade', 'disappointed to learn that'). The passive voice is used in the phrase 'concerns are viewed sympathetically' to generalise about who actually holds that view. 'Also' is used to link the ideas together in a straightforward way in this opening. Other links would be made and the main persuasive devices used in the explanation of the counter-arguments.

What other arguments might be used? How might the student continue the argument?

Practice

Now write your own response to this task.

Writing to analyse, review, comment

Example question

In *Macbeth*, Lady Macbeth explains the plan for the murder of Duncan.

You are the leader of a youth club that has been granted some lottery cash. The two main plans are outlined in the minutes of the last committee meeting.

ITEM NO	ACTIONS	BY WHOM
1	**LOTTERY GRANT £10,000:**	
	Last meeting, discussed plan to extend the computer facilities at the club by setting up an Internet café. Members should now be allowed to comment before final decision is made.	
	It was noted that some members might prefer other facilities, e.g. sports and leisure as this has been underfunded for years.	**CLUB LEADER**

Write a letter to members of the youth club reviewing the advantages and disadvantages of the proposed spending plan, suggesting alternatives. (20 marks)

Examiner's comments

*The main question is given in **bold** print and is introduced by some information that will help you to respond. In this example, you are told the **audience** for your writing (youth club members), the **purpose** of the writing (review a proposal), the **type** of writing (letter), and are given some ideas about **content** (advantages and*

Planning

Before you start you should spend a few minutes noting down some key points and deciding how you will express and organise them. Decide what the advantages and disadvantages will be and jot down some alternatives.

Content

You will need to add details about what the Internet café will offer members, explain the good points about these facilities and why they are needed. You should also consider reasons why members might not want to spend the money in that way. For example: Indicate at the end how members can express their views.

Organisation and style

You could write all the advantages then all the disadvantages.

Alternatively, you could write about the pros and cons of each idea.

This is **discursive** writing. You will need to use the features of this text type:

- mostly third person
- passive voice where it is not relevant to state who is doing the actions
- connectives of comparison and contrast ('however', 'similarly', 'conversely')
- vocabulary related to value judgements ('entirely', 'clearly').

Here is part of the response to the task written by a student

There are many advantages to the Internet cafe proposal. Members are always keen to use the limited computer facilities to do homework and play games. With the new funding, more computers would be available and they would be linked to the internet so that they can be used for research as well as for keeping in touch with friends by email. The modern equipment would be faster and funding would be set aside for ink cartridges, paper and other consummable items. There would even be opportunities for parents to use the facility during the day.

Examiner's comments

The opening statement introduces the content of the paragraph: the advantages of the proposal. The sentences are often complex so that reasons can be given concisely ('so that they can be used for research as well as ...'). The third person and the passive voice are also used ('they can be used for ...'). Opinions are subtly given in value judgements to convince the reader ('limited', 'modern').

How might the student continue?

Practice

Now write your own response to this task.

SECTION B The Shakespeare Reading Task

▶ You should spend **45 minutes** on the Shakespeare Reading Task.

▶ You will have studied one Shakespeare play and will have to complete one Shakespeare Reading Task. There will be no choice of task.

▶ The task will require you to focus on two extracts from different parts of the play. You will need to write in detail on these extracts and make connections between them.

▶ There are four focuses, one of which will be the main focus for your question:

   1 character (how a character behaves, speaks, is spoken about by others)

   2 language (the choice of words, images, style, tone and voice – and how this helps you understand character and attitudes)

   3 theme (the ideas Shakespeare explores through characters and language)

   4 text in performance (how the play is acted and/or directed).
   You will not be assessed for your written expression in this task.

1 Focus on Character

There are three main ways in which a question can focus on character.

• **'Imagine you are** … (the named character)'
   Here you will need to use the first person (*I, me, my, we, us, our* - maybe the royal plural, if it is appropriate). You will try to get inside your character, think and feel as this person would.

• **'Write about/Explain how/Comment on** … (the named character)'
   Here you will use the third person (*he/she, him/her, his/her, they, them, their*). You will explain what this character says and does and giving some opinion on how actions and words can be interpreted.

• **'How does Shakespeare present** … (the named character)'
   Here you will refer to Shakespeare himself (third person) and the ways in which he presents characters (third person again).

In all cases you will need to base your answer **closely** on the text (what is said) and the **action** (what happens, is done) in the two scenes. There will usually be comparisons (similarities) and contrasts (differences) in the two scenes.

Questions on character need some reference to other focuses, notably **language**. It is difficult to refer to a character without commenting on the way he/she speaks. Some awareness of **staging** will inform a full response.

Example

Act I Scene 7 lines 1–28 and Act 5 Scene 3 (whole scene)

Imagine that you are Macbeth.
Write about the decisions you have made and how you feel about them.

Answer 1

I went through all the reasons for not killing Duncan. I knew that his death would make me king and my ambition would come true. I went through the reasons not to kill him, because he was my king, my guest and my kinsman. I thought that there would be a judgement on me if I did it. On earth or in heaven. I know now that I've made the right decision because the witches have given me powers I can't be beaten till the wood comes to my castle and no one born of a woman can kill me so I'm safe and can't be …

Answer 2

They can't touch me, not until Birnam Wood comes to Dunsinane. The boy Malcolm Duncan's son, can't touch me either, because he was 'born of woman', so all the 'false thanes' can fly and we will never sag with doubt or shake with fear' My 'vaulting ambition' has made me king.
When I considered whether to jump the life to come, I thought that there would be problems, but I have been given supernatural powers from the weird sisters. Now things are building up. Maybe that 'poisoned chalice' could come to haunt me, but the spirits that know all mortal consequence have given me confidence Those thoughts that I had about Duncan on the night of

Examiner's comments

Read the two paragraphs which are taken from two different answers to this question. Which is the better answer?

It is clear that Answer I is quite correct in what it says and is beginning to refer to both scenes from Macbeth's point of view. However, Answer 2, in addition to showing knowledge of the two scenes from Macbeth's viewpoint, is focusing the answer clearly on text, using quotations, though not always showing them by inverted commas. One is missed out in line 3; line six begins a direct reference: 'the weird sisters' maybe does not need quotation marks, though Macbeth's own words are better than Answer I's 'witches'. The last sentence indicates that the student is going to use the past tense to refer back to the first scene – a good way of combining information from the two sections in the booklet for this particular answer, which takes you inside the head of a character. Answer 2 is paragraphed. This helps the reader focus on the points the student wants to make and gives the answer a structure.

Practice

1 Question focus: Character; Subsidiary focus: Language

Act 1 Scene 7 line 28 to end of scene and Act 5 Scene 1 *Enter Lady Macbeth* to line 60

What different impressions do you have of Lady Macbeth in these two scenes?

2 Question focus: Character; Subsidiary focus: Language

Act 1 Scene 7 line 28 to end of scene and Act 5 Scene 3 lines 1–45

How does Shakespeare present two different aspects of Macbeth's character in these two scenes?

---

2 Focus on language

There are various ways in which the wording of a question can ask you to focus on language:

- '**How does ...** (the named character)**'s language reveal** ...' quite clearly gives the key word. Your task is to look closely at what the named character says, paying particular attention to the choice of words, the way they create impressions about the character, their actions and thoughts, their relationships with other characters.

Other question rubrics which will help you spot the language focus are the 'how' questions:

- '**Show how ...**' '**Explain how ...**' '**In what ways ...?**' Individual words in the question can also direct you to a language focus. For example: *words, speech, 'what ...(character) says', soliloquy, conversation*, etc.

Remember to say what the **purpose** of the playwright's chosen words is (Shakespeare's intention) and/or the **effect** (the audience's reaction). At times the language a character uses can create **atmosphere** and build up **dramatic tension**, so look out for clues in the words that Shakespeare gives to the character.

You should feel confident that you can spot the focus in the instructions of the task. Look at all the sample questions in this section and spot the key words that guide you to the right approach.

Example

Question focus: Language; Subsidiary focus: Character

Act 1 Scene 7 line 30 to end of scene and Act 5 Scene 1 lines 27–60

Explain how the words of Lady Macbeth in these two scenes reveal different states of mind.

In these two scenes Lady Macbeth is obviously in different states of mind, almost two different people and her language shows us this. In the first scene she is talking to her husband, but in the second scene she is sleepwalking and talking in her sleep.

Her first words to Macbeth are 'Know you not he has?' This is a sharp question, really a rhetorical one, because she is saying that he can't see the obvious. This sets the tone for the rest of her conversation. She is in control and this is ironic as he is the great warrior. She uses lots of questions which are like accusations to Macbeth. She sees him as weak and uses these questions ('Was the hope drunk, ...' 'hath it slept since, ...', 'What beast was it, then ...') to make him follow her will. She makes a lot of references to courage and fear:

'Art thou afeard
To be the same in thine own act and valour'

because she is taunting Macbeth about his manhood – 'When you durst do it then you were a man;'. She uses the words 'green and sickly' to suggest that he is a coward. I think she is putting on an act when she says she will dash out the brains of the ...

Examiner's comments

Here this student quite confidently links the two scenes in the opening sentence. This is setting out the pattern for the answer and the second sentence develops it a little more. As the answer develops these ideas in the first scene, the student shows good knowledge of the text and comments on the following language features:

a rhetorical question; sentence structures – the questions; references to important thematic words – courage and fear; specific words ('green and sickly') and their effect; personal response – 'I think ...'; a reference to irony – this will be developed in a later section; tone – the way in which the words might be spoken.

In addition to these features, this student shows three different ways of using quotations to support points. Identify the different ways quotation is used.

Moreover, several of these quotations are followed by a comment on effect. This is the analytical skill which will be a feature of top answers.

Practice

You will notice that in two of these questions the word 'audience' is used. This is an invitation for you to respond to the language and/or to suggest how an audience might respond. You could make some references to versions of the play you have seen, provided that you stay with your main focus – language.

1 **Question focus: Language; Subsidiary focus: Character**

Act 1 Scene 6 and Act 5 Scene 1 lines 16–60

Explain how Shakespeare uses language to show two different sides to Lady Macbeth.

2 **Question focus: Language; Subsidiary focuses: Character and Text in performance**

Act 1 Scene 6 and Act 5 Scene 1 lines 16–60

What impressions would an audience get from the way that Lady Macbeth speaks in these scenes?

3 **Question focus: Language; Subsidiary focus: Character**

Act 1 Scene 7 lines 1–35 and Act 5 Scene lines 29–60

How do the words of Macbeth in these two extracts show different aspects of his character to the audience?

---

3 Focus on presentation of ideas

The 'themes' of the play are the 'ideas' or 'issues' that Shakespeare is exploring through his characters, his language and the action of the play. This focus brings together a lot of features of the chosen scenes.

- These three words – ideas, themes, issues – are close in meaning: they are clues in the wording of the question.
- They will often be linked with one of the 'how' question rubrics ('*Explain how ...*', '*Show how ...*', '*In what ways ...?*'
- Shakespeare's name will often be used, because, after all, he is the one who is presenting these ideas.
- Remember that the presentation of ideas is the main issue for you in your answer, so try to link the themes/issues/ideas of the play to:
- characters' words and actions
- Shakespeare's choice of words
- the relationships between characters
- the setting, staging and acting.

But, remember, these are the features that take you back to your focus – the themes/issues/ideas.

Example

Question focus: Presentation of Ideas; Subsidiary focus: Language

Act 1 Scene 6 and Act 5 Scene 1 (complete scenes)

Explain how Shakespeare explores the idea of hiding true feelings in these two scenes.

In order to trick Duncan into 'her' castle, Lady Macbeth must put on a 'false face' to hide her 'false heart'. The King immediately believes the castle to be pleasant. His first words create an appearance of beauty ('pleasant seat', 'Nimbly and sweetly', 'gentle senses') and Banquo talks about the 'temple-haunting martlet', the house martin which is a pleasant, homely bird. This is ironic, because the bird Lady Macbeth had referred to was the raven and Macbeth's castle is not a temple, more like Hell.

Lady Macbeth's words are false and very ironic, especially when she talks about service and 'every point twice done'. The audience knows what sort of service she is planning. When she says that everything is 'done double', there is a kind of echo of the witches' words 'Double, double', bringing in the theme of witchcraft. When Duncan asks for the Thane of Cawdor, he reminds of what the first Thane of Cawdor did and how Duncan was fooled by his false cover. He is going to be deceived again by the man he has made Cawdor.

The main deceiver in this scene is Lady Macbeth with her image of the 'honoured hostess'. Shakespeare contrasts her words of welcome ('honours', 'dignities', 'your highness' pleasure') and the pleasant setting with what we know is in her heart – murder. This would be a crime that Shakespeare's audience in the times of King James would see as treason – punished by death.

Examiner's comments

The opening sentence shows that this student is familiar with the play, not just the two selected scenes. The quotations from Act 1 Scene 6 are relevant and provide the base for further points about appearance and reality. The setting is used to explore this idea. Again, the words of the text are quoted and, as an extra bonus, are linked to two further images from elsewhere (the raven and the idea of Dunsinane being like Hell).

Another link is made through the language to a theme in the 'double' reference. The student picks up the point about Cawdor and his deception. There is quick reference in brackets to Lady Macbeth's words which contrast with her true feelings. Though the reference to Shakespeare's audience may not be entirely relevant, as it is expressed here, the student is close enough to a very good point about how a seventeenth-century audience would see the false face of Lady Macbeth. This answer is starting to explore the theme of falseness in a purposeful way, referring closely to language, character and setting.

Practice

1 Question focus: Presentation of ideas; Subsidiary focuses: Character and Language

Act 1 Scene 7 lines 1–35 and Act 5 Scene 1 (whole scene)

Show how the ideas of crime and punishment are presented in these two scenes.

2 Question focus: Presentation of ideas; Subsidiary focuses: Character and Language

Act 1 Scene 7 lines 1–28 and Act 5 Scene 3 (whole scene)

How does Shakespeare show the ideas of good and evil in Macbeth's words in these two scenes?

Focus on text in performance

This is the heart of studying a play. A play does not become a play until it is performed before an audience, so this should be an enjoyable task.

- Key words to look for are: '**director**', '**actor**', '**audience**', '**theatre**', '**stage**'.

- Key instruction words might be '**Imagine you are the director/actor** '.

- The words '**advice**' (noun) and '**advise**' (verb) could also be used to introduce a task on performance.

- Obviously again the '**how**' question rubrics are important and will probably be in the wording of the task.

- The ability to focus on the **structure** and **organisation** of the scenes is important. You can then think about dramatic effect and the way in which performance links to the other key issues - character, language and themes.

- Using the words 'could', 'would' and 'should' will help you put forward your ideas in a suitable way.

Practice questions for 'Text in performance'

1 Question focus: Text in Performance; Subsidiary focuses: Language and Character

Act 1 Scene 7 lines 30 to end of scene and Act 5 Scene 3 lines 1–37

Imagine you are going to direct these scenes for a performance by your class. Explain how you would want the actor playing Macbeth to show his reactions to the two different situations he faces.

2 Question focus: Text in performance; Subsidiary focus: Presentation of ideas

Act 1 Scene 6 (whole scene) and Act 5 Scene 1 line 16 to end of scene

**You have been asked to direct these scenes on the school stage.
Explain how you would want to create effects through the setting and the words spoken by your actors.**

Example

1 Question focus: Text in performance; Subsidiary focus: Character

Act 1 Scene 7 line 28 to end of scene and Act 5 Scene 1 lines 1–60

Explain how you would want the actor playing Lady Macbeth in these scenes to show different sides to her character.

The actor playing Lady Macbeth must show two completely different sides to her character. In the first scene she is in control – or thinks she is – but in the second scene she has totally lost her control and is behaving in a way that shows her tormented mind.

I would want the actor to show in the first scene that she has the upper hand over her husband who is uncertain. She should make the questions she asks – 'Was the hope drunk, wherein you dressed yourself?' – sound like accusations of cowardly behaviour from Macbeth. Her voice should be harsh with a tone of sarcasm. The words could make her sound evil and sinister, especially when she uses the horrible idea of a mother dashing out the brains of the baby. The actor should try to say the first words ('I have given suck, and know how tender 'tis to love the babe that milks me:') soft and gentle, like a mother caring for her baby, putting emphasis on the soft words. Then she should create a huge contrast when she comes to the horrid climax ('dashed the brains out'). The 'd' and 'b' should be stressed so that her voice changes and the audience is shocked. The word 'smiling' just before this should be spoken in a way that shows the audience that Lady Macbeth has some kind of twisted thread in her character. The shadows of this scene, with the lights of the banquet in the background, would add to the dramatic effect of evil being planned, so I would want Lady Macbeth to ...

Examiner's comments

The first paragraph is the introduction that gives this answer its overall structure with clear reference to both scenes. The second paragraph begins to advise with many verb forms based on 'could', 'would' and 'should'. These indicate that instructions are being given to the actor. The words 'emphasis' and 'stress' are good words of direction. Reference to voice and tone and the specific mention of the 'b' and 'd' sounds and the word 'smiling' show that this student is really getting into the task and giving close examples from the text. The final sentence makes a point about the staging/lighting and is obviously going on to say something about how the actor could use this to advantage.

Sources and acknowledgements

The publishers would like especially to thank Bernadette Carroll and Mike Duffy for contributing to the key stage 3 test material, and also John Green for his advice.

Texts

We are grateful to the following for permission to reproduce copyright material:

Age Concern and CiTV for the article "Grandparent of the Year 2002" published on www.citv.co.uk; The Agency (London) Ltd for "Going for an English" by Sharat Sardana and Richard Pinto produced for *Goodness Gracious Me* © Sharat Sardana and Richard Pinto; Amber Lane Press for an extract from "Metamorphosis" adapted from Kafka by Steven Berkoff published in *The Trial, Metamorphosis, In the Penal Colony* © Steven Berkoff 1981; Baror International Inc for extracts from *Do Andriods Dream of Electric Sheep?* by Philip K Dick; Caroline Sheldon Literary Agency for the poem "The Giant with a Taste for Mongrel Blood" by John Agard; Columbia Tristar for an extract from the transcript of *Bram Stoker's Dracula The Film and The Legend* by James V Hart; East African Educational Publishers Ltd for an extract from "The Rain Came" by Grace Ogot published in *Land Without Thunder*; Endemol UK for a transcript from *Big Brother 3*; Faber and Faber Ltd for an extract from the play "What Where" published in *The Complete Dramatic Works* by Samuel Beckett; Guardian News Service Limited for the articles "Freedom ship will be target for terrorists" by Jason Burke published in *The Observer* 28th May 2000 © The Observer and "We wouldn't put mice through this" by Mark Lawson published on www.guardian.co.uk 13th July 2002 © Mark Lawson; LKJ Music Publishers Ltd for the poem "Inglan is a Bitch" by Linton Kwesi Johnson © Linton Kwesi Johnson; Methuen Publishing Ltd for an extract from "The Jewish Wife" by Bertholt Brecht published in *Fears and Miseries of the Third Reich* translated by John Willett and taken from *Brecht Collected Plays 4* translated by Tom Kuhn and John Willett; News Group Newspapers Ltd for the article "Public enemy No1" by Mel Hunter published on www.thesun.co.uk; Oxford University Press and Faber and Faber Ltd for the poem "The Horses" by Edward Muir published in *Collected Poems* by Edwin Muir © Willa Muir 1960; Penguin Books Limited for extracts from *The Transformation (Metamorphosis) and Other Short Stories* by Franz Kafka translated by Malcolm Pasley (Penguin Classics 1992) translation © Malcolm Pasley 1992 and *White Teeth* by Zadie Smith (Hamish Hamilton 2000) © Zadie Smith 2000; The Random House Group Ltd for an extract from *A Handmaid's Tale* by Margaret Atwood published by Jonathan Cape; Trouble.co.uk/Flextech for extracts from "Gotta get thru this" by Daniel Bedingfield, "Rules of the chatroom" and Trouble homepage published on www.trouble.co.uk; and W.W. Norton & Company Inc for the poem "Imagine the Angels of Bread" published in *Imagine the Angels of Bread* by Martin Espada © Martin Espada 1996.

In some instances we have been unable to trace the owners of copyright material and we would appreciate any information that would enable us to do so.

Illustrations

Mark Oldroyd *Arena* (pages 4-5, 15), Richard Garland *Advocate* (pages 24-25), Rob Hefferan *Advocate* (pages 28-29), Venita Kidwai *Wave Digital Design Development* (page 31), Alan Down *Beehive* (pages 52, 74-75, 76), Neil Leslie *Debut* (pages 54-55), Gino D'Achille *Artists Partners* (pages 78-79, 81), Ron Tiner (pages 89,93, 94-95), Anne Wilson *Illustration* (pages 104-105, 106, 114-115, 117, 125), Johanna Holmstedt *Advocate* (pages 128-129, 132), Jonathan Williams *Arena* (pages 135, 136-137, 138), Sarah Horne *Advocate* (pages 185,186-187), Dan Alexander *Advocate* (pages 190,193).

Photographs

The authors and publishers are grateful to the following copyright holders for permission to reproduce the photographs:

Fortean (pages 2, 3); Moviestore Collection (pages 6, 58-60, 62-63, 211); Corbis (pages 26, 41, 102, 166); Rex Features (pages 27, 32-40, 43, 82, 118, 124, 127, 176, 222, 228, 233); Ronald Grant Archive (pages 66, 71); Donald Cooper (page 88); BBC Stills Library (page 141); Alamy Pictures (page 153); Arena/PAL (page 154); Camera Press (pages 158, 178-180); Bridgeman Art Library (page 173); Flextech Television (pages 240, 245, 246); Granada Television (page 248).